Dancing To The Beat
Of The Great Green Heart

Musings of an Incorrigible World-Saver

Kathryn Blume

Dedication

To all you Wild and Courageous Incorrigibles out there, and all the Generous, Open-Armed Stalwarts who support their world-lovin' madness.

You know who you are.

Forward

A friend of mine recently retired from her regular job and spent a few months visiting sustainability initiatives in the Middle East, the UK, and Europe.

Somewhere in her travels, she met the founders of Greenheart, purveyors of fair trade, eco-friendly gifts, and she brought me back a big green heart sticker as a memento.

I immediately snapped it up as a beautiful symbol of the approach we need to take in all our world-saving activities. It's an approach of inclusiveness, justice, and shining, unabashed adoration of the planet and everything on it.

While we might start lives as activists - or even just good citizens - out of fear for where the world is headed, we can only keep going - day after day, year after year, against the most heinously stacked odds and grim scientific predictions - out of profound love and deep compassion.

We must also nourish ourselves and our emerald green hearts by tell ourselves good stories about who we are and what we're capable of accomplishing.

And dancing. We always need to dance.

"To behold this hash of a creation, to take this muck and holy mess of a life, and winnow out and revel in every bit of beauty and worth that's in it."

- Glenn Berger

Table of Contents

Speeches

Vermont Public Radio
Commentaries

Star Sighting

I had a heady star-sighting last month. Actually it was more like an audience. After all, he knew we were coming to meet him – me and a couple of friends.

But, like bringing a white scarf when you go to meet the Dalai Lama, we did show up with a ritual offering of homage and respect. In our case it was carrot cake and elderberry fizz.

This recipient of our culinary kata was a tall, skinny, big-eared fellow…whom you've probably never heard of. Which means it wasn't Barack Obama.

No, his name is Rob Hopkins and he lives in the southwest corner of England in an adorable little town called Totnes.

Totnes is the hub of something called the Transition Town movement, and Rob Hopkins is the soul behind the vision.

A few years ago, Rob took a hard look at the reality of climate change, and then coupled it with the fact that, plus or minus a couple years, we are at the moment of peak oil.

Peak oil – which the US Department of Defense says we'll hit in 2012 – is the point when we've maximized worldwide oil production. All the cheap, easy-to-find stuff has been found, so demand starts to outstrip production, and the cost of oil starts to rise permanently.

Given that we use oil for everything - energy, transportation, manufacturing, agriculture, medicine – a reduction in supply, as global demand increases, will have a profound effect not just on our economy, but on almost every facet of the way we live our lives.

So, in the spirit of Fatih Birol, chief economist of the International Energy Agency, who said "We should leave oil before oil leaves us," Rob Hopkins and a group of compatriots decided to help Totnes begin the process of what they call "powering down." Powering down means relocalizing food and energy production, working to transform fossil-fueled behaviors, and increasing the community's capacity to deal with any systemic shocks caused by climate change or disruptions in fuel availability.

And thus, the Transition Town movement was born.

It's a fantastic methodology they've developed, and has a lot to do with tapping into the inherent wisdom of a community, and the belief that ordinary people have tremendous creative problem-solving capacity – as long as they know what the problem is.

Rob and his team also have a profound belief in developing a positive vision towards which people can work, rather than just giving them a big, scary nightmare from which to run. In fact, of the seven Principles of Transition, the first one is Positive Visioning, which focuses on the possibilities and opportunities inherent in what is a admittedly a deeply challenging global situation.

In only a few years, Transition initiatives have spread all over the world. Here in Vermont, we've already got about 18 different groups across the state. They're a dynamic network of concerned-yet-hopeful people striving for a resilient, engaging, and sustainable future. And they not only welcome everyone's participation, they consider it vital. Essential. Because, simply put, we are all in this together.

The We of Us

I tend to turn my head away during election season. It's just so...tacky. I mean, who decided that the best way to select our leaders was through platitudes, lying, finger-pointing, issuing oversimplified, overinflated promises, and littering our roadsides with ten thousand mini-billboards - none of which (I might add) have any sense of aesthetics or graphic design?

I do feel guilty about ignoring it. I've always believed that if I'm going to live in this world, then I need to step up and participate. And politics are an inescapable part of that. But still, something's just always felt wrong.

Then, the other day, I was poking around on line and found, back to back, photos of Tea Party rallies around the country, and an article about sustainability initiatives in Portland, Oregon. Turns out many of the projects were started by neighborhood community groups, who then reached out to partner with local government to help develop things further.

I had a thought that part of the anger of the Tea Party movement is in people not feeling like they have the capacity or resources to solve their own problems. And the mistaken assumption that those problems can only get solved by elected leadership.

Conversely, the folks in Portland have taken the responsibility of addressing their needs and realizing their visions upon themselves. They've done it by working together as a community, and then inviting elected leaders into the process.

I think a lot of political campaigns are based on promises of what I, the candidate, am going to do for you, the voter.

But, once elected, we've had this tendency to hope our leaders will "save" us. And when things remain challenging, when the big problems are still big and life doesn't seem better immediately, it's as if the hero has fallen. But more than that, it's like the powerful parent figure has failed us, the powerless child.

The irony of our current electoral climate is that when Obama ran for President, his message was "Yes We Can." We. Everyone. But maybe there was a secret hope that this guy would swoop in and save us. The truth is, though, our problems took a long time to create, and will take a long time to solve. No one person is going to "save" us. And that savior idea ultimately makes us feel powerless - then scared - then angry. And often angry at the wrong people.

Perhaps the trick is in shifting our expectations away from what we want our leaders to do *for* us, and towards who we think can work best *with* us.

Maybe a good leader is someone who creates an environment which supports people in realizing their own capacities to the fullest extent.

We need to answer for ourselves the question of what kind of a world we want to live in, and then assume the responsibility for working to realize that vision. Elected leadership is just a piece of the puzzle.

Arlo's Daughter

I don't have a long family history to recount. As far as I know, my Jewish ancestors got kicked around Europe for a few hundred years, landed at Ellis Island at the beginning of the 20th century, and promptly dismissed their grim past as not worthy of remembering.

My parents were no exception. While good at telling jokes, they weren't much for personal narrative. However, they did have a couple classic passions of their generation - folk music and liberal politics. They also loved Thanksgiving - a uniquely secular celebration which appealed to my father's die-hard atheism and his great love of a good dinner party.

One small bit of family lore I *do* know is that my maternal grandfather, Jack Soifer, was an OBGYN in Brooklyn. Grampa Jack specialized in delivering babies for lefty Jewish intellectuals, and his most famous catch was Arlo Guthrie.

My Mom and Grandmother have always considered Arlo an honorary member of the family.

So, of course, a big part of Thanksgiving in my house was the ritual of playing *Alice's Restaurant*. I heard it so many times that I know the whole thing by heart. Not just the words, but every cadence, every inflection, every little quirk of Arlo's delivery:

"Yes, sir, Officer Obie, I cannot tell a lie, I put that envelope under that garbage."

The odd thing, though, is that my lefty-politico parents never actually explained what Arlo was talking about in the second half of the song - the whole business about him trying to avoid the draft and not get sent to Vietnam.

So while that part didn't make a whole lot of sense to my young, impressionable self, I did get the distinct idea that it's good to be a smart-mouthed trouble-maker if there's something out there you object to.

More than that, I completely absorbed the concept of using the arts as a legitimate form of protest. Arlo says it himself, "If you wanna end war and stuff, you gotta sing loud." And I believed him.

I also believed him when he said, "...can you imagine fifty people a day, I said fifty people a day walking in, singin' a bar of Alice's Restaurant, and walking out. Friends they may thinks it's a movement. And that's what it is."

I believe with all my heart that this is how we change the world. It doesn't take much. Fifty dedicated people, a bar of a good song, four part harmony, and feeling.

Happy Thanksgiving.

Idle Free

OK, so quite frankly, I have very mixed feelings about New Year's Resolutions.

While it's a nice idea, theoretically, to wipe the slate clean and start the year with a fresh set of goals for personal betterment, I honestly can't say I've ever actually followed through on any of mine for longer than a couple of days. Maybe a week. Have you? I mean, be honest. How long do they really last?

Still, one can't help but hope to have some kind of impact on *something*. And one thing I do know is that it's always nice to have a buddy - you know, like a workout partner - to help you keep on the right path. Or, even better, as we all know from junior high, if everyone else is doing something, then you'll probably want to do it too. Right?

So I got to thinking, what's something that we could all collectively resolve to do together which would actually make a difference in not only our lives, but in Vermont as a whole?

And oddly enough, the first thing that came to mind was the whole issue of idling - running the car when it's not going anywhere. I know it seems like a minor thing, but until you stop driving all together, it's not. Turns out idling is a huge waste of both gas and money, and a big source of pollution.

Idling spews enormous amounts of chemicals into the air, and is linked to increases in asthma, allergies, heart and lung disease and cancer - not to mention climate change. Given that there are more than 550,000 cars and trucks registered in Vermont, reducing idling by just 5 minutes a day could cut CO_2 emissions by 50,000 tons a year.

So, what if each one of us resolves to quit idling our car, and commits to talking to five other people about it? I mean really, it's not a big state. I bet among the lot of us, we can probably reach everybody. Plus, when we run into our friends, we'll have something to talk about which makes us sound chic and trendy. We can casually mention, "You know, I've gone Idle Free." And our friends will reply, "Oh, yes! We've been Idle Free for weeks now!" And everyone feels like they're totally hip AND taking some good "low hanging fruit" kind of action - AND it's much easier than giving up, say, sugar or smoking.

We also need a slogan: How about...Idle hands may be the devil's playground, but idling cars are the devil's tailpipe. Or (for all you children of the 70s out there) Idle Free - You and Me. I'll keep working on it.

Now, to those who respond, "Well, I don't have a garage, so I only idle in the wintertime to melt the ice off my windshield,"

I say, "Invest $20 in one of those windshield covers, and then you won't have to waste any more gas!"

And to those who counter, "But I need to warm up the car," I say back unto you, "Oh, come on! You live in Vermont! Put on a hat and some mittens and warm up your car by driving it!" Even the Car Talk Guys will tell you that modern vehicles don't need ten minutes to get ready to roll.

So here's to a happy, healthy, idle-free year.

First Steps

In spite of having lived in Vermont for almost 20 years (with a little time off for good behavior), I'd never visited the Statehouse in Montpelier until just recently. The occasion was a gathering of activists rallying for bold, aggressive climate legislation.

While I didn't know what to expect from a day in the hallowed halls of power, what I certainly *didn't* anticipate was that it would be so much fun.

For one thing, it was easy. In New York City, you have to flash ID, sign in, and go through a metal detector just to get into most large office buildings. But here, in what they call "The People's House," you simply walk in the side door - just like you would at home. Of course, at home, you walk through the side door into your mud room, not into what looks like an episode of *The West Wing*, but still, you just walk in. Nobody questions your right to be there, because they all believe that it IS your right to be there.

Another surprise was discovering how many people I knew. From a Senator I first met in yoga class to a Representative I always run into in my local coffee shop to a lobbyist who's also a subscriber at my husband's theater company, it really did feel just like a concentrated version of my community - which I think, again, is the whole point.

Like Town Meeting Day, it's part of what distinguishes Vermont as a very human place. Even the most power-brokery power brokers are still your friends and neighbors, and if you bother to show up, you, too, can be part of the process of running the state.

Or, I might add, entertaining the state.

I have a one-woman show I do called *The Boycott* about the First Lady of the US launching a sex strike to combat global warming. The theme song for the show is a saucy little power ballad which demands, with rather Anglo-Saxonesque urgency, that we all cease and desist our planet-dismantling behavior. At lunch in the statehouse cafeteria (which is just like your high school cafeteria - you're always looking for where the cool people sit), a couple legislators I didn't even know came up to ask if I'd be singing this R-rated ditty in the House Chamber that afternoon.

I hadn't been planning on it, as getting arrested wasn't on my To Do list for that day. But we climate activists accidentally got into a little trouble anyway. Representative Sarah Edwards from Brattleboro had a climate resolution being read on the floor of the House, and a whole bunch of us sat in to support her and see if it would get passed.

Indeed, it *was* passed, and the climate crew in the back of the room burst into cheers and applause. Turns out, this is NOT an acceptable part of House protocol, and Speaker Shap Smith had to whackety-whack his gavel and tell us to settle down and behave ourselves. Sorry, Speaker Smith. We really didn't know.

Now, admittedly, this was a light day in the world of citizen participation. We were introducing ourselves to our legislators - and to each other. We weren't wrangling for specific legislation, battling industry lobbyists, or going toe to toe with climate deniers.

Still, as a first step in building relationships, in learning whom to talk to and how to talk to them, in learning that each of us have a place in the governance of the state, it was a great first step.

We all know addressing climate change and building a sustainable, resilient, carbon-free Vermont won't be easy. But in an era of widespread political apathy, cynicism, and divisiveness, the fact that we all left Montpelier feeling energized, hopeful, and looking forward to going back is, to my mind, a huge victory in itself.

A Dog's Life

I'm currently in rehearsals for *Sylvia*, the last show of the
season at Vermont Stage Company, where my husband is
Producing Artistic Director. Originally presented in the fall of
2002, it's the one show audiences have consistently requested
we bring back. It's also the role with which I've been most
closely associated. This, I must say, is a rather hefty irony. For
all the Great Works of Theater I've participated in - Williams,
Shakespeare, Chekhov, Beckett - I'll most likely be
remembered for a quirky little comedy in which I play...a dog.

Admittedly, it's a very funny show. And there's a universality
about dogs and their relationships to their people which most
audience members connect to quite deeply. I had a number of
folks tell me that this play actually changed their relationship
to their dog. But it's more than that.

There seems to be something about me in this role which
generates a kind of copascetic synergy. Sylvia and I, together,
are greater than the sum of our parts. Which must explain
why, for months after the first run of the show, people would
bark at me on the street, and why for years certain long-term
subscribers only referred to me by the character's name. In
fact, I had one lady say to me, "Honey, you're good in
everything you do, but you'll always be my Sylvia."

The question, of course, remains: Why? I am, I'd like to believe, not a dog, but a fully developed human being, with all a human's complexity and depth. I have more ambition than a dog, more subtlety of thought, and more variety in my food choices.

And yet, I have a vivid memory of being in the middle of a performance, audience members practically weeing with laughter all around me, and having the distinct thought: *I'm not **doing** anything here. I'm not really even acting. This is just me!* Truth to tell, it was almost a little boring.

Perhaps the key is that Sylvia isn't really just a dog either. She's an Idealized Dog, one who talks back, sasses around, and fills the void in one man's soul so completely that it turns his life upside down. She's still a pooch of simple needs - food, shelter, love, purpose - but thanks to a clever playwright, she has the capacity to articulate them very, very clearly, and without any of our human neuroses telling us we need to do something more than that with our lives.

In the end, aren't we all just pups looking for a ball to chase, a satisfying tummy rub, and a decent bowl of kibble? What more is there than loving fully, enjoying unabashedly, and serving completely? And maybe that's where the play ultimately hits home - in our desire to be that simple, authentic, and fully engaged.

One last little anecdote from the annals of dogdom: I was chatting with a woman who'd played Sylvia at a theater in Ithaca, NY. She said in one scene, the director had her sniffing the shoes of audience members in the front row. As she snuffled intently over a pair of particularly kicky cowboy boots, the woman wearing them turned to the man next to her and said, "Oh! She must smell Fluffy!"

All artifice, all convention, all theatricality completely forgotten in a moment of pure engagement, pure joy, pure belief. Just like a real dog.

The Picture of Enough

Picture that you have enough. Enough money, certainly.
Enough food, enough sustenance, enough shelter.

But more importantly than that, that you have enough love.

More importantly than that even, it's not that you *have* enough
(of anything in particular). Picture you *are* enough.

Independent from the money, the food, the sustenance, the
shelter, the love, you are whole.

Picture yourself so complete within yourself so that you never
have to act out of fear, so that every action you take in your
life is a dynamic meditation on compassion.

That sense of wholeness means you can be, in the fullness of
who you are, a mighty healing force in the world.

Because we know the world needs healing. We know the
litany of disasters, current and impending. From economic
contraction to wars to climate change to peak oil to
educational disaster to political folly.

And somehow the solutions we come up with - good, clever, powerful as they are - never quite seem to get us ahead of the tide. And often when solutions are posited, be they economic or political or technological, the resistance to them comes out of fear. The inability to act fully comes out of fear.

So I wonder if what we need isn't another piece of legislation or technological breakthrough, but a transformation of the human spirit.

What would happen if the fear was gone and we could embody enoughness?

Can you picture that? Yourself. Fearless. Knowing that you have, and you are, enough. Knowing you are compassion in action.

Can you can take that picture, absorb it, inhale into the very substance of your being? Can you picture all of us here, together, living in unabashed enoughness?

Now picture us taking it out into the world. Picture our collective embodiment of enoughness rippling out and catalyzing the very revolution in human consciousness we know we need to ensure a healthy future on the planet.

Maybe right now is the seed of our salvation.

How's *that* for a picture?

Joy and Resolve

I attended a rally the other day in support of a climate activist named Tim DeChristopher. A few years ago, at the end of the Bush administration, Tim attended an auction of oil and gas leases on publicly held lands in Utah, drove up the bidding, and managed to derail the entire proceedings - as well as protect over 22,000 acres from development. He was recently convicted of two felony counts for his actions, and faces up to ten years in prison and a $750,000 fine.

Tim knew what he was doing. He knew what the consequences of his actions could be. But he felt that risking his freedom for the sake of preserving a healthy planet was a worthwhile tradeoff. He said after his trial, "we know that now I'll have to go prison, we know that now that is the reality. But that's just the job that I have to do. Many before me have gone to jail for justice and if we are going to achieve our vision many after me will have to join me as well."

Tim's capacity to embrace his fate is something I think about all the time. I'm so deeply aware of the perilous state of our planet. Atmospheric carbon dioxide is up around 394 parts per million and climbing. We're seeing extreme weather events all the time now. The world's oceans are deeply stressed. We're facing food and water shortages and mass extinctions. The list goes on and on...

And so if you are someone who is aware of all this, who cares deeply about the fate of the world, and who feels compelled to do something about it, then you have to ask yourself the same question Tim DeChristopher asked: How far am I willing to go? How much of *my* life am I willing to sacrifice in an effort to preserve *all* life?

I ask myself those questions on a daily basis. Do I go to an organizational meeting or to a friend's birthday party? Do I fly across the country to visit my aging mother or just tell her it's Skype video chats from here on out? Or, more significantly, am I willing to get arrested and go to prison because it's what must be done for the world? Would I be willing to make a statement with my body and my freedom in order to get the point across?

The issue isn't having a felony on my record and being considered unhireable by some potential employer. I've been an actor my entire adult life. I'm pretty much unhireable anyway. I don't have kids, my husband could take care of the cats, and my paying work as a wedding officiant could easily be farmed out to someone else. There is nothing for which I'm so vital that I couldn't go get locked up for a decade or so.

Of course, I don't want to go to prison. But where do we draw the line? At what point do we say, "My love for the world is so great, and my commitment so profound, that I am willing to give up my freedom - and eat what I hear is really lousy food - because it is what must be done. And I will do it with, as Tim DeChristopher says, *joy and resolve*."

I don't know. I really don't. But I can't help wondering if at some point, life is going to demand that I find out exactly where my line is.

Days of Thunder

Ok maybe it's just me. After all I'm willing to admit having an overactive imagination. In fact I've made a career of having an overactive imagination. But I have to say that our thunderstorms of late seem different - almost scary, actually - and I am normally a big fan of charismatic weather.

But honestly, they don't seem like real life thunderstorms. They're more like something from a science fiction movie - like the ominous precursor to an alien invasion.

For one thing, the rain doesn't look like it's just falling from the sky because of gravity. This looks like rain which is plunging towards the ground because it's being pushed.

This rain is the precipitative equivalent of stampeding soccer fans trampling over each other on the way out of the stadium. Or, as my husband Mark put it, "It feels like God is hurling the rain out of the sky."

Also the lightning seems both flashier and somehow more pointed, more personal. Rather than lightning that's just happening in my general geographic area, it's lightning which appears to be specifically aimed right at me. Not that it's setting out to hit me, but I'm getting the sense that lighting wants my attention, is looking me right in the eye, and flashing expressly for my personal benefit.

Then there's the thunder, which is definitely...I think the technical term would be "boomier" and more sustained than any thunder I've ever heard before. It roils and stomps and plunders its way along. It's a very ominous, bullying kind of thunder, willfully throwing its weight around to make sure we know who's in charge.

And not only that, but if there were a message contained in this storm, if the storm were actually talking, then the thunder would be its voice. And I've been starting to wonder exactly what it might be saying.

So as the latest bank of apocalyptic doom clouds rolled in, I recorded a chunk of the thunder, and ran it through Google's new Audio Translate feature. What came out was:

"Oy! What a fever I've got! When I find the mamzer who put all this shmutz in my atmosphere, I'm gonna give him such a zetz on the keppeleh!"

This, of course, can mean only one thing: Mother Earth is my Grandmother. Known as Mama Beattie to both friends and family, she ruled the roost - dominated it, really - from the comfort of her tricked out pink barcalounger, and God forbid you should make her mad enough to get up and come after you.

Mama Beattie did not mince words. Neither did the voice of this storm, which I guess we can call Big Mama Beattie. Big Mama Beattie went on to say things like: "I have had it with this mishegas! Stop it with the buying useless crap and throwing it away!" and "Who left the tap on in the Gulf?" and "Fracking schmacking!" and "Hey you kids, quit blowing up my mountains for coal! Don't make me come over there!"

On and on it went - a beefy litany of complaints about our reckless eco-behavior and utter failure to keep our planetary room clean.

And it's got me worried because...well...while I didn't translate the whole storm, I have the distinct feeling that Big Mama Beattie may be getting up out of her chair.

Thoughts from the Bus

Sunday morning, as the rains from Tropical Storm Irene began to pummel down, a group of Vermonters boarded a big tour bus. Paid for by donations from friends all over the world, this bus would carry them south for 10 hours to Washington, D.C.. Armed with banners, business suits, Obama 08 campaign buttons, and 30 plush toy planet Earths, their goal was to follow fellow Vermonter Bill McKibben and almost 400 other concerned citizens and get arrested outside the White House.

These arrests, part of a two-week campaign of direction action, protest a plan to build a pipeline which would carry crude oil from the Alberta tar sands all the way down to refineries in Texas.

I can imagine that as they drove past areas of the state about to be inundated by flood waters - some for the second time this year - they were probably thinking about a couple of things.

Some were probably thinking about those rising waters, hoping their friends, colleagues, and communities would be ok. Hoping that there would be enough money, elbow grease, and stamina to clean it all up. Again. Wondering how many times this is going to happen - again and again - as global temperatures rise and extreme storms become more and more common.

Some were probably thinking about *Petropolis,* a documentary film about the tar sands shown at a fundraiser for the trip a few nights before. They were probably thinking that "tar sands" are such a benign-sounding name for the gigantic industrial strip mine which has been scraping the boreal forest away, chewing up the bones of the earth for oil, and which already emits more carbon dioxide than all the cars in Canada.

Some were probably thinking about a report issued by the State Department a couple days before they climbed on the bus. This report said that the pipeline project would have "limited adverse environmental impacts."

Some were probably thinking about a comment made by NASA's chief climate scientist James Hansen. Hansen said that if the pipeline is built and the tar sands are fully developed, it would be "game over" for the climate.

Some were probably thinking about President Obama, in whose hands the permit for the pipeline lies. They were probably thinking about his acceptance speech when he won the Democratic nomination in which he said people from the future would look back and see that "this was the moment when the rise of the oceans began to slow and our planet began to heal." They were probably wondering what happened and why they even needed to be on that bus in the first place.

Some were probably thinking about the act of getting arrested and the combination of fear, anticipation, joy, resolve, determination, desperation, commitment, devotion, and love embodied by all the other people on that bus.

And some might not have been thinking at all. Some might have been singing. Some might have been singing a song taught to them the night of the benefit, a song from the Yoruban people of Nigeria, a song which is quickly becoming the anthem of the climate movement. *Ise oluwa, kole bajey o,* which translates as: "That which the creator has made can never be destroyed."

Ise oluwa, kole bajey o.

Let's hope so.

Essays

Lemon Pledge

The Pledge of Allegiance is screwed up. Deeply. Hopelessly flawed.

Let's look at it again so we're all on the same page:

> I pledge allegiance to the flag
> Of the United States of America
> And to the republic for which it stands
> One nation, under God, indivisible,
> With liberty and justice for all.

What an enervating crumb of dopey doggerel. It's an amateurish poem and a lousy promise. Can you imagine if people got married that way?

> I promise to marry
> The ring on your finger
> Which is attached to your hand
> Which is at the end of your arm
> Which somewhere along the line
> Becomes you, who I love.

The POA's best part is at the end, but by the time we get to the chunk which could raise our pulse, we're already thinking about lunch.

Who wrote this sawdust, anyway? I've always suspected either some Jeffersonian wannabe – an 18th century AV geek from the social backwaters of the Continental Congress who got tossed the writing job as a Bone of Pity, or a committee of reluctant right-wing revolutionaries who wanted some sort of mind-numbing oath of unquestioning loyalty so that we wouldn't have too much freedom and liberty poisoning the minds of the newly independent populace.

Not so. Not even close. Turns out (and this is going to bunch the undies of all kinds of oath-loving, under god-protecting conservatives) Our Friend The Pledge was written in 1892 by Francis Bellamy – a *socialist!* Well, a Baptist minister Christian Socialist, but one who was interested (according to his biographer Dr. John W. Baer) in "a planned economy with political, social and economic equality for all." He wrote the POA during his tenure as a committee chairman for the National Education Association. As it happens, he really wanted to include the word "equality" in the pledge as well, but he knew that the rest of the committee was opposed to equality for women and African-Americans. Oy!

Not only that, but, as you may know, he didn't include the phrase "under God" in the original POA. That was added in 1954 following a Supreme Deity Inclusion Campaign undertaken by the Knights of Columbus, a change Bellamy's granddaughter says he would have resented. Lest you doubt this, note that Bellamy left his Boston church under considerable duress in 1891 thanks to his socialist sermons, and quit attending his Florida church because of the rampant racial bigotry.

Bellamy's lefty leanings aside, 112 years later, the POA has all the zip and pizzazz of a rainy day at the slug farm. I mean, for starters, *I pledge allegiance to the flag*? It's a *flag*, a symbol, and a pretty abstract one at that. Now, I get that some people are into symbols: crosses and stars and polo ponies and alligators and gigantic, gas-glutton, faux-military, pollutomobiles (a symbol for the large phalli they wish they had). But that flag bears about as much relation to the actual United States as the zeros and ones in the code of a digital snap of the sun bear to the actual flaming ball-o-hydrogen, source-of-all-life in our sky.

While we all know that the stars represent the states, most people probably don't know what the stripes and colors represent. I didn't. And after a quick trip to the Betsy Ross home page at ushistory.org, I discovered The Awful Truth: "There is no official designation or meaning for the colors of the flag." The only person to take a whack at it was George Washington, who, in a moment of what could only be hemp-inspired grandiloquence, said that the stars came from the sky, the red "from British colors" (whatever that means), and the white stripes symbolized seceding from England. Cosmic thrills and chills from the dude with the wooden teeth.

Back to the Pledge.

And to the republic... Ok, that just sounds too much like
"Republican," and we're all way too het up over the Son-
Dunce Kid's Hole-In-The-Head Gang to get anywhere near
that one. Why don't we wait until we find us some real
compassionate conservatives before we start trying to
rehabilitate the R Word.

Nevertheless, let's finish the sentence: *to the republic for which it
stands.* Now we're getting somewhere. We're about to
describe our country, i.e. the thing to which we're pledging
our allegiance. Except, who knows what pledging allegiance
actually means? It's vague. It's like saying, "Support our
troops!" With what? Lycra? Be specific!

Moving right along: *One nation.* Ok. Duh. Got that.

Under god. This is problematic for a whole lot of reasons, but I
think I'll hang my hat on the separation of church and state as
put forth in the First Amendment of the Constitution (which
is, by the way, a kick-ass document, and you should read it
sometime) and leave it at that.

Indivisible. This is clearly theoretical. I mean, really, around
which particular issue are we all united?

With liberty and justice for all. Finally, we're getting
somewhere. But like I said, by now, we've already taken a
Sudafed and fallen asleep operating heavy machinery.

This baby definitely needs an Extreme Makeover. So, let's start by asking the question: what is the point and purpose of the Pledge in the first place? What is it used for – other than to get school children going on their day with a nice, meaningless group drone? I have no idea. I went to a little hippie high school in Oregon and never had to take a civics class, much less chant the POA. But I think it has something to do with re-affirming our commitment to citizenship, civic responsibility, and the ideals such as liberty and justice (and equality), upon which this country was founded. Which is nice.

To tell you the truth, though, my real concern over the POA – apart from thorny issues of ennui and aesthetics – springs from the slippery slope down which Pledge could easily slide. There has been too much corralling of loyalty, patriotism, and "what it means to be an American," by Red-Blooded Poseurs threatened by anyone who doesn't follow their authoritarian rule-set and ossified belief system. I fear the POA will get turned into some kind of narrowly defined metric of Homeland Loyalty, and that certain Powers In Power will start to *strenuously* demand unquestioning support for their behavior.

Honestly, I don't think having a national allegiance or loyalty is a bad thing – if it's a conscious and re-negotiable one. It just needs to be about loyalty to the *country*, not necessarily the *government*. The Declaration of Independence (another fine read) states that governments get "their just powers from the consent of the governed." Which means none of us should be required to swear a blind pledge of faithfulness and obedience if we don't consent to, for example, a misbegotten, unjustified, militaristic, imperialist rampage. The POA is good, in that it requires us to give some thought to the terms of our civic responsibility – ideally to the land and to each other – but it was never intended to make individuals abrogate their forebrains in service of idiotic and dangerous leadership. We are not the Borg. Resistance is not futile – in fact, when things are going astray, it's required, and the POA should reflect that.

Ok, now we know what we're doing, so let's get to the re-write. First, let's change the title. I'd like to swap "pledge" for "promise." We all know what "promise" means, and what it feels like when one gets broken. No kid ever says, "Aww, Dad! Why can't we go to the zoo? You pledged!"

Allegiance is a tricky word. Technically, it has to do with fidelity and loyalty, and in some cases, obedience – but that starts to be a problem when you run it up against the ideas of liberty and disagreeing with your government. So, let's just call this thing The Promise. Or, how about The American's Promise, since that's what this is really about – what we, as Americans, promise, as citizens of this nation, to do on behalf of the country and each other.

Turns out, it's a really hard thing to write. My first draft came out looking like The Progressive's Manual for Utopian America:

As a citizen of the United States of America,

I promise to nurture and cultivate the democracy by voting in every election and working to protect the integrity of the voters and the electoral process (and see what I can do about getting rid of the lobbyists);

I promise to remember that democracy and free-market capitalism do not automatically go hand in hand, and to work for viable alternatives to our current system which has left millions of people without well-paying, meaningful jobs (and left about 5 people ridiculously wealthy);

I promise to uphold the ideal of Equality by working for equal pay for men and women and equal access to affordable health care (including stuff related to contraception and family planning because that's nobody's damn business but their own);

I promise to uphold the ideal of Liberty by vigorously protecting the First Amendment and politely respecting the Second Amendment - but not going overboard about it since we all know the Founding Fathers didn't anticipate AK-47s and shoulder-mounted anti-aircraft weapons;

I promise to uphold the ideal of Justice by transforming
our revenge-based penal-industrial complex into a
compassionate system founded on principles of
prevention and rehabilitation...

Et cetera. I could go on for pages regarding what I would love
to have each and every American promise to do. But that
would be A) overtly partisan; B) supremely idealistic; and C)
hard for school kids to recite. We want everyone to think
about this, right? We want this to be something everyone in
our ideally indivisible land can relate to.

Gandhi says be the change you want to see. I think that's
good. Let's try it from there:

> As an American,
> I promise not to be an asshole.
> I promise not to be a greedy bastard.
> I promise not to be a heartless, power-hungry
> egomaniac.
> I promise not to be a short-sighted idiot.
> I promise not to be a selfish prick.

Sigh. Alright, let's go back to the juice. The core. Bellamy
was on to something, even if it came out sounding like verbal
Valium:

> As an American Citizen,
> I promise to uphold our ideals of

Liberty, Equality, and Justice
By treating others as I would like to be treated;
By cultivating compassion for the people I don't
understand;
By respecting the people with whom I disagree;
And by sticking up for the people worse off than I am.
I also promise to ask for forgiveness if I hurt someone,
and offer forgiveness if I am hurt by others.
All this goes for everybody in the world, not just
Americans.
I know it's going to be hard, but I promise to give it my
best shot.
Good luck, everybody.

Well, at least it's a start. I haven't figured out how to slip in
stuff about yoga, meditation, and living an ecologically-sound
lifestyle, but maybe I get can get that into a re-work of the
national anthem.

Strength

My husband Mark's theater company is undergoing tough times right now. A perfect storm of both long and short term financial stressors, combined with sudden staff losses, have made their future look more than a little precarious. It's an odd juxtaposition, because they've actually been doing extremely well. Subscriptions are up, ticket sales are strong, audiences love the shows, and the work consistently receives rave reviews in the press. Actors and designers enjoy working there because Mark creates an atmosphere of safety and respect where artists feel free to do their best work. It's really an amazing little company.

In strategizing their recovery, both Mark and his board are having to undertake some rapid maturation, and learn to overcome their fear of The Ask. Fast. It's not an uncommon fear. It takes a special type of joyous, hardened soul to constantly encourage people to open their wallets, and doubly so in moments of crisis.

In the past, the board has been insistent that they come to The Ask from what they call "a position of strength." And yet, in order to achieve Maximum Ask Impact in this critical moment, they must also convey the gravity of the situation. The paradoxical question du jour seems to be *how do you convey the simultaneous truth of strength and weakness? Abundance and need?* The uncertainty of how to do it can be paralyzing – even when they know that not asking at all will result in only one unfortunate outcome.

Still, no matter how imperative, it's a hard task to juggle. Part of what's tough is that both realities are simultaneously true, and they must be balanced. Convey too much strength, and you diminish the true depth of your need. Show how much the blows have hurt, and you might repel assistance. As one potential donor and board member expressed, nobody wants to jump on a sinking ship.

Their salvation, I think, is going to come from both celebrating what's truly remarkable about the company, while acknowledging where mistakes have been made – not to lay blame, but to display maturity and learning. If they can articulate the arc of growth in their knowledge and experience, display the map of the potholes they've stumbled into along the way, openly admit their weaknesses and how they've learned to transform them, that will convey the true strength.

It won't be strength from force and will, but from humility and wisdom, which, bolstered by immediate financial assistance, will keep the company vibrant and viable for many years to come.

But more than that, they need to challenge the common assumption that strength sits diametrically opposed to need, and that need itself automatically connotes weakness. It's an absurd myth that anyone can actually go it alone, and yet this culture reverently cultivates that myth and allows it to be the very crucible in which our most cherished legends are born.

It's interesting having all this reflected in the light of the Presidential election, our relationship to the rest of the world, and the kind of leadership for which people so piquantly ache. We are so afraid of our own imperfections, so threatened by paradox and ambiguity, and so mortally terrified of being weak. Being wrong.

We've been in a fight-or-flight response for three years now, perpetuated by an administration and media which irresponsibly continue to stoke our fears, rather than dare ask the hard questions of why things are the way they are, and – more to the point – what responsibility we might have in the situation or what mistakes we might have made.

The deep fear, of course, is that if we admitted any responsibility or fallibility, if we were honest with ourselves about our past behavior, we might lose any claim to being a right and righteous power, and somehow, like a child, think we deserve our pain. We're so scared to look at the truth, we're actually in a state of simultaneous fight and flight. I've heard it called "learned helplessness," though often it feels like plain freaking out to me.

How else to explain the vast numbers of undecided voters or the people who claim to disagree with everything the administration has done, but continue to support the President because, "he's a Christian" – no matter how serious, well-documented, and unchristian-like his behavior. How else to explain the clenched, vitriolic partisanship, and the sense that winning a Phyrric victory would still be fundamentally better than losing an honorably run race.

How do we raise our children? We tell them to be honest. We tell them to admit their mistakes. We tell them it's ok to fail, because that's the only way you learn. We tell them to be kind and share and not to hit or steal. We tell them to have love and compassion and to do unto others... We have told them, but we have not taught them. That kind of teaching can only happen by mature example.

We think we will never tolerate doubt or failure or mistakes in our leaders, but when have we ever experienced that degree of honesty, or truth, or open-hearted revelation? When have we ever allowed them to be human? Perhaps we couldn't bear it. It would be like the moment in adolescence when we realize our parents aren't perfect. At first we hate them for it – partly because it forces us to grow up, and test the limits of our own strength. Ultimately, it's exactly what we need.

So, perhaps that's what we need to do now, for ourselves and this beloved, confused, convulsive country, which suffers so profoundly from a massive case of arrested development. We need to grow up, and assume the mantle of true strength and inspired leadership. We must find a maturity born from the capacity to embrace pain and ambiguity with patience and grace. It's time for each of us to take a long, deep breath, and consciously ease ourselves into adulthood. It's time to choose the only path which will assure us our survival.

Elephants Declare War on People

So my inspirational source here was an article in the *New York Times Magazine* about how all across Africa and India and Indonesia, elephants are basically going postal and attacking humans and gang-raping rhinos.

It's all happening because elephant society is naturally close-knit and complex, and by killing tons of elephants, we have decimated their social structure. And while it may be a fallacy that elephants are afraid of mice, it's true that elephants have a very long memory – they have the memory of, well, an elephant – and now they're mad as hell and they're not going to take it anymore.

I didn't really want to talk about this. I wanted to publicly declare my undying love for George Clooney (who just won the American Cinemathique award), and reveal my plans to become a movie star so that I can buy a small island in the South Pacific, kidnap George Clooney (and Bono), and have a righteous lefty love triangle in my hideaway island paradise.

Of course, that's only going to work until my island – like the tiny island nation of Tuvalu – gets inundated by rising water levels and absorbed back into the sea, and we have to relocate, which is what all the Tuvalans are currently doing.

Which is really the problem here. Elephants going apeshit is just the symptom. Fucking up the planet is the problem.

Causing 20,000 species a year to go extinct and CO_2 levels to rise higher than they've been in the last million years and melting ice caps and increasing the number of dead zones in the world's oceans and slaughtering half the hippos in the Congo in the last two weeks alone is the problem.

And even though climate change is a totally accepted fact worldwide (except by Senator Inhofe of Oklahoma who chairs the Committee on Environment and Public Works and thinks global warming is a communist conspiracy), and even though general scientific consensus is that we have about ten years – max – to really address these problems before everything goes to utter hell...

Well, actually, maybe everyone doesn't know all this. Maybe some of you haven't heard or aren't convinced or think that Al Gore made it all up to elbow his way back into public life. Maybe some of you wonder, "Hey, hasn't the earth's climate always varied incredibly widely? What about the ice ages? And weren't things all steamy and palm-covered and Florida-like during the age of the dinosaurs?"

Well, look kids, in 1988, the World Meteorological Organization and the United Nations Environmental Programme created the Intergovernmental Panel on Climate Change to evaluate the state of climate science. In its most recent how-we-doin' assessment, the IPCC unequivocally stated that human activity is drastically altering the world's climate.

And, all the major scientific organizations in the US whose members work directly on these issues: the National Academy of Sciences, The American Meteorological Society, the American Geophysical Union, and the American Association for the Advancement of Science (AAAS) – they all agree with those conclusions.

Now the naysayers say, "Hold on a sec, we don't understand all the mechanisms and feedback loops and all the important details about this global warming "controversy."

Well, first off, the word controversy is just crazy-denier marketing language. Like the timber industry calling an old growth forest "over-mature" and referring to clear-cutting as "tree density reduction" in order to create a "temporary meadow."

Maybe we don't know every single last detail about global warming, but brain surgeons don't know everything about the brain, and they seem to be doing ok.

And the truth is, there's no controversy among all the people who study this. All of them say that the atmosphere is heating up because over the last 150 or so years, human beings have been burning fossil fuels and increasing the atmospheric load of carbon dioxide and other greenhouse gasses, and exacerbating things by doing an awful lot of tree density reduction.

One more thing about the deniers. Britain's national academy of science actually sent a cease and desist letter to a certain corporation responsible for giving $2.9 million to 39 different groups who work to deny the science of climate change. Who is that corporation? Our old pals at ExxonMobil, who've been nailing over $5 billion in quarterly profits from the sale of what? Oil!

So naturally, I am just a little tweaked about all this. I feel like Frodo in *Lord of the Rings*. And you know, now that we're talking LOTR, Viggo Mortensen can come to my little island love nation, too.

Anyway, Frodo didn't want to get sent off to save Middle Earth. He didn't ask for that responsibility.

And that's how I feel! But the truth is I'm a very ambitious woman and worldwide ecological collapse would totally blow my chances at becoming a movie star.

Which is why we gotta fix this. It's why we gotta protest the fact that our Energy Secretary just picked the former CEO of ExxonMobil to develop solutions to America's energy crisis.

Which is why we've all got to find a way, like Frodo, to accept the truth of what's been handed down to us by our dear Uncle Bilbo. We have to face the fact that drastic climate change is really happening – fast – and we're causing it. We have to find a way to say, "Ok, I get it, and I'm going to help solve the problem."

And it's got to be all of us. From the commie tree-huggers to the right-wing nutjobs, and everyone in between. Because this is not a partisan issue. It's not a political issue. It's an issue of planetary preservation. No controversy, no more argument, end of story.

Though if any right-wing nutjobs here happen to have George Clooney's phone number, I'll let you argue with me just a little bit more.

The Jeans Dilemma

This has to do with how I'm seeing the world right now. It's divided into two camps: Things Which Help and Things Which Send Us Down The Crapper. It's like at my gym, there's a basket of disposable plastic razors on the counter as a courtesy to the members, which is very nice of them, but I look at it and all I see is a little tub of unbiodegradable planet death – only slightly worse than the disposable razor heads I use at home or all the pricey wax and waxing strips and other painful waxing accoutrements which get tossed in the garbage every time I'm looking to avoid 5'o'clock pit shadow.

But this isn't about the ecological impact of smooth, hairless underarms. This is about jeans.

I love to wear jeans. Who doesn't? But I also know that conventional cotton, from which jeans are made, is a highly toxic proposition. It's grown with lots of oil-based fertilizers and pesticides, none of which are good for you. In fact the EPA considers seven of the top 15 pesticides used on U.S. cotton crops to be "possible, likely, probable, or known human carcinogens" – and all of which deplete the soil poison our ground water, and kill far more wildlife than just cotton-munching weevils. So, basically, cotton is hardly, as the ads say, the "fabric of our lives." It's more like the fabric of our demise.

Not to mention that the denim from which jeans are made has almost certainly been dyed, emitting chlorine, chromium, and other pollutants into the environment. Plus, the processes by which they texture jeans – stone washing and so on – involve pumice, which has to be mined. Also not good.

Then there's all the shipping materials around the world, stuff made by toddlers in Chinese sweatshops which are powered by coal-fired plants, so you know coal, CO_2, global warming, blah blah blah… Basically, when it comes to jeans, we're talking many large paving stones on the road to Armageddon.

So, then, the earth-conscious casual dresser thinks to turn to organic cotton and hemp. The thing is, at least in Burlington, there's only a couple places that sell green jeans, as it were. You can also order them on line, but then here comes the hard part.

I've read that the average woman has to try on 50 pairs of jeans before she finds one that fits, and I'm no exception. I'm short and curvy. I have a 28 inch inseam, a small waist, and a bottom which, as Freddie Mercury would say, makes the rockin' world go 'round.

And, I find that most "fashion-forward" organic cotton and hemp clothing (as opposed to burlap-sack-hippie-mamma-organic-cotton-and-hemp-clothing) is cut to fit the waiflike and anorexic proportions of teenage girls. So the idea of ordering a pair of jeans which would probably fit quite nicely on my arm, then sending them back, ordering new ones, try on, send back, repeat *ad nauseum* seems like a time, money, and energy-wasting task of Sisyphean proportions.

So what's an eco-gal to do?

Well, whatever an eco-gal *could* do, THIS eco-gal just broke down and bought a couple pairs of conventional cotton jeans which fit well and look great. I figure I'll wear them for years, and I just try to ignore the creepy, Love Canal sensation crawling up my legs.

I justify this flagrantly unenvironmental behavior by the fact that I shop almost exclusively at consignment stores – that's clothing recycling making up the majority of my wardrobe. And yes, I admit to some really big cancer-causing-chemical denial here, but I am just not so perfect a human being that I can deal with EVERYTHING. My Buddhist friends tell me to take the middle path. But I'm not really a Buddhist. I'm more Buddish.

I suppose another answer might be that I diet and exercise to the point where I can fit into the waiflike and anorexically proportioned earth-friendly jeans, but then we have a serious feminist problem replacing our ecological problem, and I've only just accepted myself as I am (mostly) and I will NOT willingly return to the Fallujah of Self-Esteem. Or the Battle of the Bulge. Pick your favorite war. And I'm *totally* not ready for any Gandhiesque weaving of my own diaperwear.

Ok, so now I have a couple pairs of carcinogenic but fabulously ass-friendly jeans. They are, however, too long. So I hem them. Fine. Easy. No problem. But now I have four six-inch-long denim tubes I have to deal with. I guess you'd call them my toxic assets.

I believe in recycling. I believe in cradle-to-cradle design. I believe that nothing should ever become just waste, just garbage. So what do I do with these? I can't throw them away, because then we have a solid waste problem. I could toss them in my compost pile and hope that as they decompose, my backyard won't become a superfund site.

But these bits of denim also contain Lycra - not likely to become one with nature within the next few millennia. So, into the scrap bag they go, hopefully to see another life as a patch on...something. Or a quilt square for when civilization collapses and, like pioneer ladies of yore, I am forced to make my own bedding.

Perhaps the whole problem could be avoided by not wearing jeans in the first place at least until I find some green ones which fit. But give up jeans? The 4-season, dress it up dress it down, hard-traveling, easy-washing, disco to garden, socialite to redneck, banker to bull-rider, Moscow to Mexico City, ripped or creased, Sharpied or Sequined, high waisted, muffin topped, skin-tight, boxer-baggy, Levis or Luckys, cradle to grave wondergarment??? Fuck!!!!

Well, we are talking about the future of the planet here, and the whole issue of ecological footprint, and I'm not sure my few personal acres can support the whole denim-based sartorial struggle.

I don't have any easy answers. Maybe by the time I need new pants, there will be a wider range of organics available to me. Or I'll have worried about it so much that I'll have lost the weight needed to fit into the teeny-weenie jeanies.

But really, I think it's time to move from pondering these issues into making some bold choices; changing my thinking, so that *any* choice I make – no matter how problematic or awkward it might seem – is no longer problematic or awkward if it's a planet-based decision. After all what do I love more? Displaying my beautiful shiny hiney or having a healthy world? It shouldn't even be a consideration. Like wearing seat belts or not littering. You don't think about it – you just do it because it's the right thing to do.

Just. So much easier said than done. Well, I suppose I shall take the Buddish path, keep scootching myself as far to the ecologically pure side of things as I can, and hopefully, as our culture and economy change, the far side will soon become the middle.

And THEN I can tackle my armpits.

The Art of Action

I'm always struck when well-known actors and musicians are ridiculed for participating in some aspect of the political process. Think Meryl Streep testifying in front of Congress to ban Alar on apples or Tim Robbins and Susan Sarandon protesting the war or Angelina Jolie serving as a goodwill ambassador for the UN. Frequently the public reaction runs along the lines of *what do a bunch of dumb actors know?* Or when Natalie Maines spoke out against Bush people told her to just shut up and sing.

To be honest, I'm more than struck, I'm tweaked. Or more than tweaked, I'm infuriated. I'm an actor. Since when did my choice of career abrogate my responsibility as a citizen? Since when did my choice of career cause my brain to leak out my ears? Clearly never, that's when (Though I will allow for making fun of Harrison Ford waxing his chest hair to demonstrate the pain of tropical deforestation. That was just silly.).

But really, if artists are just dumb and harmless, then why, when fascism strikes, are we first up against the wall? Why were so many actors and writers and musicians and painters vilified by the House on Unamerican Activities Committee? Why was Victor Jara murdered during the military coup in Chile? Why did Hitler ban Ernst, van Gogh, Chagall, Picasso, and Cezanne?

The truth is, we're not harmless, and we're not dumb. As Susan Sarandon said, *"People should fear art, film, and theatre. This is where ideas happen. This is where somebody goes into a dark room and starts to watch something and their perspective can be completely questioned...the very seeds of activism are empathy and imagination."* In other words, we're potent and powerful and dangerous in a wonderful, world-changing way.

It's something I became convinced of following my experience as Co-Founder of the Lysistrata Project. In early 2003, right before the US attacked Iraq, my friend Sharron Bower and I organized over 1000 readings of the ancient Greek anti-war comedy *Lysistrata* in 59 countries and all 50 US states.

Both immediately afterwards and in the years since, I've had the great fortune to hear from numerous participants, many of whom spoke of their participation in terms of re-validating their artistic careers – or, more specifically, that it was a renewing of their sense of relevance as artists. And I've been hearing a lot more discussion lately in academic circles, conferences, and activist groups, about the vital role that the arts can play in galvanizing people to awareness and action.

The act of reading a play as a form of protest was also important, in that it gave people who were disinclined to march in the streets or write letters to the editor or call their congressperson a means of expressing themselves in a way which felt both pointed and playful, but still entirely non-confrontational. Lysistrata Project participants also felt their voice multiplied exponentially by their awareness of thousands of other people doing exactly the same thing at exactly the same time. And, it was flat-out fun - something with which activists aren't immediately associated.

In a recent edition of *Yes Magazine*, the editors posed the question: "What happens when we throw off the invisible chains that keep us from realizing the world we want—when we, as they say in the global south, decolonize our minds?" That's a wonderful question, but we've also got to consider exactly how that happens. How do we learn to see the invisible chains, how do we rattle them, learn to throw them off, and then how do we know what kind of a world it is that we want?

Here, I think, is the greatest purview of the artist. And it happens on a couple different levels. Art shows us the world as it is, names the true-but-as-yet-unnamed. Art allow us to see ourselves, our whole selves, in infinite shades of dark and light. Art reflects ourselves back to us in an intense, highly concentrated, extremely potent, and sneakily digestible form. Often, we connect and relate to what we're seeing and hearing in a work of art long before we recognize our actual selves reflected back. We get surreptitiously trapped in a vision of truth. And once we see, it's very difficult to un-see. It's hard to walk away unchanged.

I've had many audience members come up to me after performances of both *The Accidental Activist* (which told the story of Lysistrata Project) and my current global warming show *The Boycott* and tell me that I'd just articulated out loud ideas and feelings which they'd been experiencing, but hadn't expressed – either to themselves or other people.

Many people have a kind of fear/guilt response to their more powerful emotions - thinking that they shouldn't feel as much or as powerfully as they do, and that if they acknowledge the depth of how they feel, then they might be overwhelmed or destroyed by their emotional experience. I know what it's like to work so hard to contain and deny my inner life that I'm left paralyzed, with no energy to take any kind of action. Seeing your inner life played out truthfully and unabashedly on stage validates and legitimizes the potency of your feelings, releases the energy locked up in the emotional containment field, and allows it to be put to far more productive, proactive use.

There's also a magical, alchemical element to the artistic experience, something dynamically and inherently elevating. There have been times when I've gone to, say, a fantastic Frederic Chiu piano concert or brilliant Bill T. Jones dance performance and not only lost myself in the experience, but lost any sense of distinction between myself and the artist. For a moment, I was Frederic, I was Bill. I walk away having absorbed from them a touch of the divine, believing that I might actually become my best self. And for a moment, at least, I feel that I am. I feel that I'm walking in the borrowed shoes of genius and inspiration, and that right now, anything is possible.

We need that kind of exhilaration because of the truly murky problems we're facing, and how challenging they're going to be to overcome. We need to believe, every now and then, that we are capable of anything.

This, of course, begs the question: what, exactly, are we capable of? And herein lies another gift artists bring to the table. We live in a world of imagination, a world of not-yet and never-been. We are capable of creating – from glistening filaments of dreams and wonderings and other milky mindstuff - whole and real and concrete worlds. We specialize in overleaping the reality of what is and delving deeply into the could be. It's vital to be able to do that, to shine a light in the murk. It gives us a hopeful, inspired vision to move towards, rather than just a raging, dark fear from which to run.

Love Letter To Bill T. Jones and Company

I was asked to be part of a post-show discussion after a presentation of "Blind Date" by Bill T. Jones. We were given a videotape of the show ahead of time so that we could prepare our response to the piece, and this is what I wrote.

A Love Letter to Bill T. Jones and His Gang
In The Middle of This, Our Blind Date

January 15, 2006
The Stage
Flynn Center For the Performing Arts
Burlington, Vermont
United States
North America
Earth
Milky Way Galaxy
Universe (or one of 'em)
Eye of God, Womb of Goddess, or Back of Turtle – you pick

Dear Bill and The Gang (and I am hereby claiming the word "gang" for describing peaceful collectives, just as I am re-claiming the word "theatre" away from describing any place where war is being waged),

First off, I really hope this is a good letter, because I doubt I have the strength or the stamina to make love to each and every one of you individually.

Second, I just gotta say to Bill: I loved the military-industrial complex pas-de-deux. Wicked clever. You totally earned your MacArthur on that one.

Ok, so, Everybody – Bill and The Gang – this has been a great date so far. You're really smart and funny and creative and HOT and I think we have a lot in common.

And believe me Bill, I completely understand your conflicted feelings about smoking. It really is this weird hybrid – a bad habit crossed with a powerful addiction…and a little something else. Something totally easy, kind of gross, falsely reassuring, and just a wee bit too enjoyable for our own good.

Sort of like our acceptance of war. We have <u>so</u> been meaning to cut down, and somehow, we never quite do. We never manage to break that habitual, half-conscious choice to fire up. To fire back.

Now, I know conventional wisdom would say that violence is inherent in human nature, and these evolving phases, these generations of war, are the inevitable result.

But I don't buy it. Do you?

(I guess this is where we, as Folks On A Date, have to figure out if our values mesh enough for hope of a long-term relationship.)

I mean, I'm not a naïve loony, I know violence is inherent in human nature, but must it be inherent in human culture? We can choose nurture over nature. I have to believe we can. I have to believe that sooner or later we're going to be brave enough, mature enough, wise enough to say, "You know what? We're done. War is just not an acceptable option anymore. We know choosing peace is going to be hard and dangerous and we're going to make mistakes, and blood will most likely be shed, but we'll probably make a whole lot fewer mistakes and shed a whole lot less blood than if we keep bombing the snot out of each other, so listen up people because This Is It! We're stealing back the crescent moon! Deal with it!"

And this is why (and I hate to say this on a first date 'cause it makes me sound really needy and stalkerish), but this is why I love you. Why I hope you'll call me. Soon. Because I think what you offered up tonight, what you said with your bodies and danced with your voices and sang with image after image was an athletic, audacious, precarious defiance of the inevitability of war. You've made the outrageous choice that no matter what happens, you will side with peace.

You know, I think we're already at the point in the dating process where we have the Big Talk about What We Really Want.

Why not? So, here's what I want. Remember that guy who wanted to see more rage on stage? Of course you do. Well, me too! But I don't mean victim rage. I don't mean powerless, consuming, collapse-into-my-bed rage. I mean warrior rage! But I don't mean violent, striking out, vengeful warrior rage. I mean love-warrior, dance-warrior, song-warrior, truth-warrior, drum-warrior, leaping yoga warrior rage – and you did that! That's what blossomed up flew out flooded thundered and shattered my heart tonight!

That's why we're so perfect for each other!

In fact, I want to see MORE more rage on stage! More rage that we have accepted endless, insidious, inexorable war. More rage over election-stealing and fundamentalist-courting and SUV-driving and global warming-ignoring and poor people-screwing (that's poor people *getting* screwed, not screwing each other) and patriotism-co-opting!

I want loving, brilliant, in-spite-of-our-fear rage that spills off the stage – and this is a little retro/60s/Living Theatre of me I know – but I want it caroming like a medicinal force of nature, like the holy, healing version of a natural disaster. I want a righteous, sanctified, unstoppable lovequake that will thrum us out of our disastrous fake yellow boxes of security, wash over us in a mighty wave of benediction, pour out of our mouths in a sacred vow of hope and send us – right now – into the streets shouting, "We can start over! We can start over! We can start anew!"

See, this is why I get a little nervous on a blind date. I know I can be slightly intense. But so can you! Another reason why we'd be so good together!

I should wrap this up. I don't want to overstate my case.

You know, I don't know the day The Duck of Death will come quacking for me. That's a date to which I am happy to remain quite blind.

I hope that it's an endless, perfect day. I hope I die for all the right reasons, wearing the best red dress in the world. Maybe, if I have time, I'll even shave my head. Because the bald girl dancer looks very, very cool like that, and I would *love* to die looking cool.

But even if it's for no reason at all, or if it happens on the Vanishing Point Day when war has become indistinguishable from peace, and civilians from soldiers, and the field of battle from the whole wide beautiful world, I will offer up my soul and consider it a life well-lived if – just once – I have nourished a heart, a stage, a tiny unrecognized country with a speck, a flick, a moment of the gravity-defying, back-bending, star-spangled hope that you've given me.

I don't know if we have a future together, Youall and I. But for now, right now, here at the end of this blindingly magnificent date, I promise that when you dance, I will dance.

When you speak the truth, I will repeat it. When you hold out your hand, I will take it. When you walk, I will walk along in time. And when you call out, I will catch you when you fall.

With one sweet kiss, I wish you good night.

Love,

Kathryn

Observations From a Day 50 Years From Now

I might be surprised that I made it this far. After all, ninety-one is still considered something of an achievement, especially given what we've lived through in the past half-century.

Except for the fact that all the women in my family seem to break the tape at 100 without much effort, and then sail on past the finish line for another couple of years before dying, I think in large part, because they're ready for a new suit of clothes and another great adventure.

Good thing I've been doing yoga all these years. I can still do a headstand, touch my toes to my nose. Things they applaud you for when you're 5 they'll oddly applaud you for again a lifetime later.

I think the part which surprises me the most is how glad I am to still be here. Not that I've ever *wanted* to die. I've always wanted to live forever (if forever could be a little less wrinkled and creaky).

Except there was a moment – one of those vivid, almost cinematically remembered moments – when I was 20. I was in Seattle, sitting at the table in my boyfriend's kitchen. An ocean-blue wall on my left. Brad breakfasting across from me – his eyes a perfect cerulean match for that wall. Ooh. Brad. Seventy damn years and a couple dozen men later and still, with a single thought, I can feel him. Moments like that let you know for sure that time is just a made-up thing.

Anyway, I was reading Seattle's alt-weekly paper… Oh, hell. Now I've really just dated myself. I'm talking about a free periodical, printed on a paper called newsprint, which came out once a week and covered the doings in the city from an edgy, artsy, lefty perspective.

So, the Seattle paper's lead story was about this book that had just come out. It was by an unknown guy named – get this – Bill McKibben! Yup. Years and years before the Presidential Medal of Freedom, the Nobel, the knighthood, all the streets and schools named after him, the statues in all the parks. And this book was announcing to the world the reality of a thing called global warming. We'd never heard of it, and it was almost unimaginable. The ice caps melting? Islands and coastlines disappearing like Atlantis? Mass extinctions on an unthinkable scale? Drought? Resource wars? World-wide starvation?

I think that's probably what's hardest for you young folks to understand. How fast things changed once the feedback loops really got going. It really wasn't always like this. Kids sometimes ask me, "Why didn't you know?" Of course we knew. Intellectually. But we liked our lives as they were and the world seemed a pretty immutable place. It took a lot of what I call "convincing-by-disaster" for people to believe we really could wreck it that much.

But this Seattle paper was trying to talk about it, and they did a little sidebar piece about what Seattle would look like once the ice caps melted and the whole city was under twenty feet of water. They had a drawing of the Space Needle, this 600 foot tower, half-submerged.

And I looked at that picture, and I thought, "I have no desire to see that. None." That was the first time I didn't want to live forever.

But you don't have to live forever to see a lot of things you never hoped to see.

So why am I glad I'm still around? Why am I glad I've got at least another 10 years?

Because as everything we'd been warned about started to happen, as the world cracked, so did our hearts. And when your heart cracks, you can either die of grief, duct tape it together and solider on, or you can let all those cracks and open spaces get filled up by love. It's like cracks in cement. Water gets in there, and things start to grow. Life happens in those cracks. The same is true for us, and it's an amazing thing to see.

Things could have gotten so much worse. But we finally woke up. We finally got startled and scared by the idea that we are just a bunch of critters living on one tiny, miraculous rock in space and we have absolutely nowhere else to go. We finally realized how much we love our little rock, and we finally decided that it was worth being unstintingly selfless and heroic and creative and courageous in order to save it. And ourselves.

And in that moment, we came together as one people. You could feel it in the air. You could see it in the eyes of strangers when you walked down the street. As scared as we were, there was also a kind of marvelous, miraculous determination which settled in. We really and truly changed. We grew up. We adopted, as a global people, that beautiful old Jewish concept of *Tikkun Olam* – repairing the world. We made it our creed, our manifesto, our purpose.

It's like some kind of Zen parable – having the thing you want least to see result in the thing you want most to see. I don't understand why it has to happen this way but that's Life for you. And we've still got such a long way to go. But I'll keep watching and keep pitching in – bearing witness and bearing the load – until it's time for my new suit of clothes and another great adventure.

I Believe

As a climate activist, someone who spends the bulk of her time trying to awaken the community to the realities of climate change and peak oil and enliven people to do something about it, it's very easy to focus on where we've gone wrong. It's almost effortless to bemoan the amount of destruction we humans have heaped upon the planet.

I have no problem alternating between fear, despair, and rage when I contemplate how many climate tipping points we've crossed and how close we are to losing the planet's ability to support life and civilization as we know it. It's so easy to feel both flabbergasted and powerless in the face of our apparent lack of passionate, gung-ho readiness to do something about it.

Despite the remarkable spectacle of people in 181 countries creating 5200 events for 350.org's international day of climate action on October 24, despite the pole-to-pole call for strong action and bold leadership on the climate crisis, I am deeply influenced by the doubt most experts express at the ability of the delegates at this December's international climate conference in Copenhagen to walk away from the table with a solid, science-based, toothy climate treaty in hand.

I want more than anything to believe we are capable of addressing the climate crisis, and in fact I do believe more than anything that we're *capable* of it. I'm just not so sure we're *willing* to take it on. Why? Because the reality of addressing the problem involves profoundly scaling back from the lives we're currently leading.

We are a civilization which has built its foundations upon fossil fuels. We use them to get us to the corner store and we use them to get us into orbit. We use oil to make everything - from asphalt to aspirin, deodorant to duct tape, vitamins to volleyballs. We use fossil fuels to build our homes as well as light and power and heat them. Oil is the mainstay of commercial agriculture's pesticides, herbicides, fertilizers, and antibiotics – and oil drives all the machinery and equipment used to grow, harvest, process, and distribute our food.

The reality we're facing is that not only does all this industrial and agricultural activity pour carbon dioxide and a host of other greenhouse gasses into the atmosphere and heat up the planet – which is bad enough – but we're also facing the fact that we have maximized global oil production. This is known as Peak Oil.

We're not running out of oil *per se*, but it's getting harder to find and more expensive to produce. Which means that all the elements of our society which have been based on cheap oil and the massive amounts of energy contained therein are going to get much more expensive as well – prohibitive to the smooth running of the global economy as it's currently structured. Or, as Dr. Fatih Birol, chief economist with the

International Energy Administration, recently stated: "We must leave oil before it leaves us."

But here's the thing: I don't blame us. We may have wreaked incredible havoc on the planet, but we didn't *mean* to. In fact, I'm in awe at the depth and breadth of humanity's creativity and ingenuity. We found a mess of black sludgy stuff in the ground, and look what we've done with it!

In fact, I look at what humanity has created during the vast scope of our history, both pre-oil and during this little energy boom, and I'm blown away. We've made paintings on grains of rice and built rockets to the moon. We've made cathedrals and tinker toys and spandex and haute cuisine and Rock and Roll and the Hubble telescope and iPhones and sneakers and giant Buddhas and pyramids and mummies and illuminated manuscripts and samurai swords. We built the towers of the World Trade Center and then tightrope-walked between them. We research and dissect and explore and learn and dance.

So, what do I believe? I believe that if we can harness ourselves, we can clean up the mess we've made – even now, at the 11th hour. More than clean it up, I believe we can re-make the world with a constructive power that rivals and even surpasses our destructive power. I believe that even in a carbon-constrained world, we can have remarkable lives of novelty and meaning and humor and adventure and purpose and fun and love. I believe that in 20 or 50 or 100 years things probably won't look anything like they do now, and that the shocks to our collective system and the changes to our way of life will be challenging to absorb at first. But I also believe that we are incredibly courageous, infinitely creative, and supremely adaptable, and I believe it is our moral responsibility to step up to this task placed upon us. It's up to us. There is nobody else.

I also believe that no matter what happens, there's meaning and value in taking action, in being part of this chapter of humanity's story. Because in all likelihood, something or someone will survive. And whatever the conditions of their life are, whoever they are, I would want them to know that someone tried to hold things together on their behalf. I would want them to know that someone was thinking of them, living there, farther on down the road. I would want them to know that someone, whoever they were, didn't give up.

Copenhagen Revisited

I have been meaning to come out of the closet for a while now, and confess that I took a very different view of what happened during COP15, the UN climate talks in Copenhagen than what has become the oft-repeated mainstream story of unmitigated failure.

I spent the bulk of my time in Copenhagen not watching the UN negotiations at the Bella Center (though giant kudos to all the activists - in particular the folks from Climate Justice Fast - who permanently lodged themselves there), but at Klimaforum.

For those of you who missed it, Klimaforum was a gathering of over 7000 people from global civil society – activists, artists, educators, farmers, freelance journalists – all coming together to talk about climate change, peak oil, and environmental justice.

It felt as if the whole world was there. I met Kenyan tree-planters and Ecuadoran Indians and Navajo social workers and Lapland Elk herders and Tibetan liberation activists. I met a Swiss shaman with a 20-foot alphorn, a Brazilian tour guide in body paint and a leopard print bikini, a handful of Danish Hare Krishnas, and not one, but two Santa Clauses.

Klimaforum had over 300 scheduled events including talks on topics ranging from preventing rainforest destruction to dismantling industrial agriculture. There were workshops on permaculture, canceling Third World debt, and Transition Towns. There were youth activist trainings, spiritual rituals honoring the climate crisis, and networking rooms for sharing ideas.

There was art, music, and theater – including my own solo show *The Boycott*. Many of the folks who couldn't get into the overcrowded Bella Center ended up at Klimaforum and I eavesdropped on several discussions about how "this is what COP15 should have been."

Concurrent to COP15 and Klimaforum were two other convergences: a conference of world mayors sharing cutting edge urban planning techniques and technologies for reducing CO2 and increasing sustainability, and a gathering in the anarchist neighborhood Christiania of indigenous leaders (cheekily called the Climate Bottoms) working on their own tactics and solutions.

On my daily travels through Copenhagen, I was blown away by all the public art, youth activism, bloggers by the truckload at the extremely well organized TckTckTck media center, hundreds of thousands of people marching through the streets, and the endless how-do-we-fix-it conversations in all the restaurants and cafes.

In spite of the fact that for weeks beforehand the official word was that there wasn't going to be an agreement coming out of

COP15, we all still wanted a miracle. Of course we did. Climatically speaking, the hour is very, very late indeed. And thanks to people like Ian Fry, Chief Negotiator from Tuvalu, and President Mohamed Nasheed of the Maldives, there were at least a few dramatic mini-miracles out there.

But honestly, the real miracle for me was watching global civil society say, "While the people at the Bella Center are leaders, they are not the only leaders. Our capacity to address the climate crisis does not rest solely in their hands. We have passion and vision and immense creativity. We have profound love for the planet, and for each other. We have a vision of universal justice and the ability to collaborate across cultural lines, and that's exactly what we're going to do."

I came away feeling - and still feel - the strength and power of the movement in which we're all engaged. To echo Transition Town Maestro Rob Hopkins, I feel an intense sense of both humility and gratitude for being present at this remarkable, charismatic (and yes, sometimes terrifying) moment in human history. And I bow my head to the remarkable global community working like hell to weave us all a future we can anticipate with joy.

Speeches

The Four Pillars of Creative Action
Keynote Speech for
The Convergence of Artists Activists, and Educators

I am gobsmacked. Flabbergasted. What an incredible gathering. And, I'm deeply honored to have been asked to speak to such an amazing group of people.

Now, first off, I have to say that I would talk about Lysistrata Project, but I only have five minutes for this, and I can barely say my name in five minutes much less talk about Lysistrata Project. I think I'm going to have to bend the rules of time and space for this one no matter what.

I also realize that "The Four Pillars of Creative Action" is a little phallic, but during Lysistrata Project, my co-founder Sharron Bower and I (and I'll talk about Sharron a lot) called our organizers "Spearheads." Which was also rather phallic, but we simply reclaimed it for ourselves. So, we'll just reclaim pillar as well, because quite frankly, "the four ova of creative action" sounds a little silly.

Finally, to conclude my preamble, I'm offering these brief ideas up as observations. I'm not trying to be the Dr. Phil of the Artist/Activist/Educator – otherwise known as the Artivator – community. I'm not trying to be Dr. Phil. Yet.

Ok, Pillar 1. Imagination/Love/Inspiration

Big ideas and emotions are great. Inspiration is invaluable – utterly essential so that we're not always reacting against bad stuff, but proactively working towards the world we've been dreaming of. It's why artists are so valuable – to show us the world as it could be.

We need love because it's a better long-term fuel than anger.

However, many projects fall prey to what I'm going to call the "This Little Light Syndrome." And it goes something like this. Feel free to join in.

> This little light of mine, I'm gonna let it shine
> This little light of mine, I'm gonna let it shine
> This little light of mine, I'm gonna let it shine
> Let it shine, shine, shine...

> *(Long Pause)*

> Ok. Now what?

Or they fall prey to my personal favorite:

> This little light of mine, I'm gonna let it shine
> Til it becomes a big, huge, titanic light
> That washes evil from the hearts of men
> Saves the world
> And makes me rich and famous

> And then I'll finally get to redo the house
> And backpack through Europe

Or, something completely different:

> Wow. Look at that injustice! I'm feeling really pissed!!
> I bet I could fix it.
> But the bad guys always win.
> So, I'm going back to bed.

So to get anywhere, we need Pillar #2 – Structure.

In many communities – artists in particular – the word structure has the same resonance as the word *Castor Oil*. Or *Republican*. But, we all know that in reality, that's how you get anything done. Small tasks. Clearly defined roles and goals.

Sharron grew up in a hard-core Right Wing Texas military anti-abortion Eagle Forum family (as opposed to me, a lefty Jew from Oregon who now lives in Vermont). And what she learned is that's a big part of why the right is so effective. They're all willing to buy into structure. They go over the top, but there's a lesson there.

Lysistrata Project had loads of structure – we just redefined it. Redefining structure is a big part of what I admire about the Dean Campaign.

Think *Power With* and *Power Under* as opposed to *Power Over*. I'd define those, but I only have five minutes and I'm adhering to the structure.

Pillar #3 – The Self.

This goes back to that Marianne Williamson quote: As you liberate yourself, your presence automatically liberates others.

You have to deal with your own personal wounds and baggage because it has an effect on everything you do, how you interact with people, how you deal with stress and conflict – which is ALWAYS going to come up.

During Lysistrata Project, we kept telling people don't serve your career, serve the cause, and we still had turf wars in Chicago, Seattle, and Minneapolis. People forgot they were supposed to be preventing a war.

Sharron and I ran into all kinds of drama, plus we had an 11th hour interpersonal conflict – two, actually, which could have ruined everything. But because we were two people who'd been trying to do our emotional work, we kept communicating, served the project, got through it, and stayed friends.

Oooh! Dirt! Now don't you *really* wish I had more than 5 minutes?

Plus, when you work on yourself, you cultivate your capacity for empathy and compassion. So that when someone is having a temper-tantrum, caught up in their ego and fear, you can step back and be the adult in the room.

Pillar #4 – Faith.
Ecumenically speaking, it's faith that anything is possible, and that everything counts. Everything matters. It's faith that while you can't control the outcome of your project (and really, you can hardly control anything), something will happen that will probably have a positive effect on someone's life.

You often don't get to know who or what, but something. And it counts, and it matters.

To conclude, here's some proof that anything is possible:

Once upon a time, there was a ship captain whose job it was to sail his boat to Africa, load the boat with people, and bring them back across the ocean to be sold into slavery.

One day, in the middle of the ocean, he woke up. He realized that those were people in the hold of his ship. And he turned around and took everyone home and spent the rest of his life writing hymns.

He didn't end slavery. But still, what he did, that one act – that counts. And his most famous hymn is *Amazing Grace*. And that's had a huge effect.

So, just remember: You are all acts of amazing grace. And you all count.

Amazing Graces

Keynote speech for the inauguration of Jane Blume as
President of New Mexico Women in Communications

Ok, before we get rolling, I want you to grab one of your business cards and put it on the table in front of you. We'll get to it later, but better to have it at the ready now.

Done? Good. So, hello everyone! I'm very happy to be here to help celebrate the presidential re-installation of... You know, I don't know what to call her, this just-anointed fearless leader of yours. She hates it when I call her Jane – I tried it once in high school and got grounded for a month. You'd think I could get away with it *now* – after all I am almost 40, and you hope getting older has got to count for *something* useful, like being able to call your mother by her name. But I know how she feels about it and it's her event and so far be it from me to ruffle any Maternal Feathers.

I suppose I could call her Mom, since of course she *is* my mom and you all *know* she's my mom, and that would be clear and fine... But for the fact that I have absolutely no idea what kind of relationship you all have with *your* mothers (or with your children for that matter). As a therapist friend of mine once said, you're hard-wired to your mom and it's nigh well impossible to break that connection, and so for some of you, the very word MOM, at each and every utterance, might conjure up some associations which will render this event a somewhat less-than-pleasant place for you to spend your time, and we're supposed to be here for a celebration – and have some *fun*.

And while of course I intend no negative associations whatsoever with the word mom or the concept mom or the job of mom, or anything momly-related, goddess forbid I nevertheless inadvertently step into the quagmire your own personal mom-o-rama, thereby kicking you into five more years of therapy just because I got the inside track on this nifty public speaking gig in Albuquerque and momed my way all over the place without considering the wider social implications.

Not to mention the fact that we *just* celebrated Mother's Day and who knows what kind of brunch you might have had? You might just now be getting over that hangover. So best, really, I think not to go there at all, yes?

So let's call her Jane Blume, which is a little more…broadly, generally referential…and I promise to call her Mom once we get home. Like the Buddhists say, take the middle path.

Anyway, I want to commend you on a wise choice for your once and future leader. Jane Blume is a phenomenally successful woman. And while one could endlessly enumerate her myriad talents and accomplishments, the aspect of her *modus operandi* on which I'd like to focus – perhaps an unexpected one – is how much she helps people for free.

It happens all the time. People call Jane Blume. They ask her for help, for advice, for ideas – for who knows what all... ancient bagel recipes from the shtetl, the governor's private phone number, her opinion on whether logos printed on thong underwear would be a good marketing tool for a high occupancy, medicare-funded assisted living facility – and she always happily, cheerfully, generously complies. With absolutely no expectations of return or *quid pro quo*.

Now, some harder-nosed, more traditional – one might even call them more patriarchally-oriented – business folks might accuse her of giving away the farm. Or of undervaluing the worth of her own knowledge and expertise - or even just her time.

But I'd submit to you that what's really going on is that Jane Blume understands the difference between social and fiscal capital. She understands that investing time and energy and intellect and compassion in people is just as valuable an investment as putting money in the bank. And she understands (and makes choices based on) this difference while living in a culture which tends to value, or more significantly, tends to prioritize short term monetary gain and the accumulation of wealth, power, and material goods over almost everything else.

It's a reflection of a culture still in its adolescence - though we're beginning, collectively, to understand the consequences of not thinking in the long term. Or at least we're being unavoidably faced (particularly in the realm of climate change, which is the issue horse I currently ride) with the need to make mature, thoughtful, visionary choices now in the hopes of positively influencing a highly uncertain future.

But I'm not here to wallop you upside the head with the 2x4 of climate change. At least not yet…

* * *

I want to get into that difference between social and fiscal capital. And I want to get into the idea of enough. I want to posit the notion that you can have enough money: enough to take care of yourself, your kids, donate some, put enough away for retirement. You can have enough stuff. Enough books, cars, clothes, collectible doohickies on your shelves. In fact, you can probably – easily – have much, much less of all of that and still live a fruitful, meaningful life.

But I also believe that as much as you can have enough money, you cannot have enough social capital. You cannot have enough goodwill in your community, enough kids getting a great education, enough clean air and water, enough affordable health care, enough peace.

Except in our adolescent society, we actually say the exact opposite. We say that while not all the different groups in our community get along, they get along…well enough. And that while not all kids have access to a good education, enough of them do – however many that is. Enough people have affordable health care and decent housing – even though more and more people don't. Enough people have clean air and water. We have enough peace.

It's a dangerous bargain to make – and it exacts a cost on all of us. It engenders a kind of persistent, low grade fear that at some point, we might find ourselves on the wrong side of the equation. On the wrong side of enough. We might fall through the cracks. We've seen it happen, time and again. Sometimes it happens to us. But when (most of the time) it doesn't, we knock on wood or wipe our brows in relief and whisper, "There but for the grace of God…" Though given how many people are falling through the cracks these days, it would appear that the grace of God is in pretty short supply as well.

And the only way to inoculate ourselves against that low grade fear and build an impenetrable reservoir to protect us from drought of God's grace is to have more – much more than enough money.

And when you're spending your time making money – hoarding it – for fear of your own safety, then you don't have much time to consider the well being of anyone else. When you're in fear, you're in a perpetual state of fight or flight. You're operating from your brain stem, your lizard brain, and when you're in Lizard Brain Mode, you end up making fear-based, short-term choices, which you might not ordinarily make if you were operating from your higher, more mature self. You know, like for example, you go into Lizard Mode and you end up electing a Lizard President. No offense to lizards.

And just so we're clear, I am so *not* talking about electing WICI President Jane Blume here.

* * *

Ok, I realize my political slip is showing, and quite frankly, Bush-bashing seems almost a little passé these days. Except for the fact that while for some of us he's a nightmare we'd soon like quickly to forget (or if you voted for him, an embarrassment you'd like quickly to forget), we dare not forget the reasons he came to power, nor the consequences of his tenure in office. He's going to be leaving a huge mess that will take years to clean up, and each of us will have to shoulder that burden consciously. Willingly. And with compassion for the bad choices which have been made.

At any rate, the big question remains: How do we engage – and change – the Enough Paradigm? How do we address – head-on and without fear – what seems like an endless litany of totally overwhelming problems? And then on top of all the regular issues we have to deal with, there's that old 2x4 of global warming (some call it global climate catastrophe), which makes everything else look like a minor ingrown toenail on the foot of the great green goddess Herself.

Well, Gandhi said be the change you want to see. Marianne Williamson said, "as you liberate yourself, your presence automatically liberates others." The trick is to have the courage to live with a sense of abundance, with a sense of enough, in spite of your fear. Have the courage to make choices based on no-strings-attached generosity, in spite of that lizard-brain desire to flee the big, hairy wolves at the door.

As communications professionals, you're in an incredibly exciting position to not only help your companies and clients live in generosity and abundance, but to help them model it for lots and lots of other people – everyone who interacts with them or gets their message. What an amazing opportunity you have – each and every day – to be the change you want to see. Not only that, but to imagine the world as you would like it to be, and then act as if that world is already here. Or at least pretty darn close by. Right by your ear. As Arundhati Roy says, "Another world is not only possible, she is on her way. On a quiet day, I can hear her breathing." And you can help give anyone who might be suffering from a lack of imagination – or hope – the chance to hear that breath. Feel it, warm, on the soft skin of their neck.

That Other World – she's, perhaps, the best mother of all. One we'll never, ever have to roll our eyes at in adolescent frustration or feel obligated about taking out to brunch on a day which (if you weren't aware of this) was originally designed not as a celebration of individual motherhood but as a day when mothers would rise up as an unstoppable force for peace.

Maybe that's the way to transform the whole Mom Issue. For mothers, all, to climb off the celebratory pedestal that one Sunday in May, and take to the streets instead.

* * *

At any rate, you, as communications professionals, have the great good fortune to spend your days communicating the wildly exultant possibilities of that other world. You can offer hope and the paradigm of abundance.

What's truly exciting about living in the time we do – crazy and perilous as things are – is that the internet provides us easy access to information sources outside the mainstream. There are myriad places available on line where we can not only tell our own stories, but take the time to get our own batteries recharged. Read about all the amazing, dedicated, not-mentioned-in-People-or-Time activists and artists and educators and business leaders who are working to make the world a better place.

The children of that softly breathing other mother world are walking right in front of her. Out in the streets. Paving the way.

Let me finish by telling you about one of them – though I didn't read about him on line. He's my husband, Mark.

Mark runs a little regional theater in Burlington. Vermont Stage Company. And in the past 6 years of his tenure there, he has not only pulled the company back from the narrow, crumbling edge of total ruin (which is a whole story in itself), he has also made it his singular priority to run the company according to his values: treat his artists well – house them in lovely places and pay them as much as he can and tell them repeatedly how much he appreciates their contribution. He makes it a priority to select plays he loves, which challenge audiences intellectually and emotionally, lift their spirits, and transform their lives, rather than just do shows that will guarantee an abundance of (as we say in the biz) butts in seats.

He treats his subscribers the same way. He tells them how much they're valued. He believes in complete transparency and writes fundraising letters telling people exactly what's going on with the company – the triumphs and challenges. He explains why he makes the creative choices he does, and why his donors are so valuable. And people actually *like* getting his fundraising letters. They like reading them! And how often do you hear about that? Really, how often do you get a fundraising letter that you actually read?

It's still not easy. Just because you're doing wildly transformational art with people operating at the height of their craft doesn't mean anyone's going to show up. They're doing *Who's Afraid of Virginia Woolf* right now. It's an incredible production. Could be the best they've ever done. Gorgeous set. Exquisite performances. Amazing reviews. And it's just not selling. Turns out the show is a little too rough for many of our emotionally tender Vermont audiences. Also, many people have the image of the movie in their heads, which is just dark and raw and bleaker than bleak. The Vermont Stage production isn't like that. Sure the play is about drunk people being extremely unkind to each other, but it's also got humor and love and the poignancy of a desperate couple trying – yet one more time – to reach out and connect with each other. But that's a hard thing to communicate to people who have Elizabeth Taylor and Richard Burton screeching in their heads.

The hardest part is that they're taking a huge financial hit from this. And for a company which two years ago almost closed its doors and operates very, very close to the bone, there's just not much wiggle room for this kind of loss.

While it won't sink the company, it seriously jeopardizes next season's big, wowzy, never-done-anything-like-this-before project – a production of *King Lear* with live Taiko drumming and starring a vibrant, 85 year old Broadway veteran who wowed the pants off us last year playing Niels Bohr in *Copenhagen*.

Vermont Stage was going to have to raise an unprecedented $20,000 extra – on top of the regular budget – to make this happen. And they were ready to do it. But now, with the $10-15,000 loss on *Virginia Woolf*, it seems like an unimaginable – not to mention fiscally irresponsible - task.

So what's an artistic director to do? Mark briefly considered re-mounting a wildly successful production of *Our Town* from a few years ago. For sure it would sell like the proverbial hotcakes. But he'd be doing it purely for financial reasons, and really, a re-mount would feel to him as much like backsliding as the financial losses from *Virginia Woolf* do. It would be a fear choice, and artistic soul death.

He could pick another show – a 2-4 character living room drama much cheaper to produce. But *Lear* already has him so excited. Has audiences excited. The universal response when he says he's producing *King Lear* (after he says, "Yup, that *King Lear*") is, "Wow!" How can he possibly give up the Wow Factor?

So the plan? He's taking it to the streets. He's writing another of those open-book fundraising letters which says, *"Here's what just happened – why I chose Virginia Woolf and why I think it didn't sell. Here's what we want to do next season. Here's how much we need your help to do it. And if, by September, we still don't have the money to do Lear, then we won't. But it won't be for lack of trying, and it won't be for lack of asking."*

It's a very human approach. He's not selling, he's just telling. The good and the bad. And it generates a true sense of partnership with the community. He's saying, "We're not us doing this for you, but we're all of us doing this together." He's abandoned spin for truth. That's Mark modeling his Other World. Scary and hair-raising as it can be, he wouldn't – couldn't – do it any other way. Just like President Jane Blume (who Dad and I think should be running for another kind of President...But I'll leave it to you ladies to form that particularly exploratory committee.)

* * *

So. To conclude here, I'm going to offer you a little task, a little assignment. I humbly suggest that you help each other rise up, all you women communications professionals. Time to grab your business card – so go ahead and grab it – and hand it to the person on your right.

Now, what you're going to do is go home today, and write down three goals you'd like to achieve in the name of being the change you want to see. Three things you'd like to do to liberate yourself and make that other-mother world a reality. Could be anything. I don't care. Buying organic produce or dumping an icky client or putting all your publications on recycled paper or working pro bono more often or (my personal favorite) getting rid of your SUV and all your incandescent light bulbs and lobbying for clean energy and better mass transit.

And then, whatever your three goals are, you're going to call or email the person whose business card you just got and share those goals with her. And that person is going to call or email you back and tell you how great those ideas are, and cheerlead the heck out of the situation, and together, you're going to make that troika of transformational dreams a reality.

And every time you come back to a WICI meeting, you're going to share your progress with the group. And the job of President Jane Blume here is going to be sharing your successes with the good people of New Mexico and with WICI chapters all over the country. And you will all feel very, very good about yourselves and sleep very well at night and perhaps you will become known as New Mexico WICI – The Mothers of Transformation! And it's going to be FUN!

So good luck, and Great Green Goddess-Speed!

Thank you.

Art, Activism, Inspiration, and Muffins
Speech for Seidl Lecture at the
University of New Hampshire at Plymouth

How many of you guys played patty-cake as a kid? You know, hands clapping up down, etc... Ok, well here today, we're going to start off by playing a little patty-cake. And if you think that this is a game for 8 year old girls...think again. We're talking EXTREME PATTY-CAKE here.

RULES:
1. Everyone Participates
2. No talking
3. If all else fails, improvise

Now, what if the goal of patty-cake were to, say, reduce the amount of carbon dioxide in the atmosphere? Think about that for a sec. If we could get this patty-cake right, we could reverse global warming. So, let's try it again.

Obviously, patty-cake won't solve our problems. But this little exercise mirrors the path we have to take in the work we need to do in the world.
- Get as many people as you can together for a common purpose
- Have a strong investment in outcome
- Overcome shyness, embarrassment, lack of rhythm

- Crazy ideas and risks might net unexpected results and insights
- Need to listen, look each other in the eye and work together
- Work with what you have – even if you're clapping in the air

At this point, you might be wondering: yeah, but where did the title of this talk come from? Art, Activism, Inspiration, and Muffins?

Well, we're a world that needs to see some action. On a lot of fronts. And action's more fun when it's fun. I just saw U23D up in Montreal, and THAT was a perfect example of the marriage of art, activism, and an insanely good time. Although after seeing it, I have to admit that it is possible to get too close up to Bono. At least when he's 60 feet high in 3D.

* * *

Now, I should back up a moment. When you start talking about activism, it means that you're talking about addressing some problem in the world. And one of the hardest things to deal with in life is to take in the cold, bottom-line truth about how challenging most issues are, how many immediate crises need your direct attention, and how difficult it seems to succeed. Particularly now, given the global scope of most of the challenges we're facing. And it's important to know what's going on and instill in yourself and others a sense of genuine urgency and responsibility.

But how do you do that without depressing people so badly they'll just shut down on you? What? Global climate crisis? Advancing tropical diseases? Oceans rising? Mass extinctions? Hand me the Haagen-Dazs, I'm going to bed. Overwhelm and burnout are very, very easy things to fall into.

Perfect example of complete burnout was Cindy Sheehan, whose son Casey was killed in Iraq. She got involved in, and became a leader in the movement to end the war. She bought a piece of land in Crawford, Texas, called it Camp Casey, and demanded to talk to Bush. Ultimately, she ran out of money, damaged her health and her personal relationships, and gave up, very publicly, in an open letter to America, where she said:

> "I will never give up trying to help people in the world who are harmed by the empire of the good old US of A, but I am finished working in, or outside of this system. This system forcefully resists being helped and eats up the people who try to help it. I am getting out before it totally consumes me or anymore people that I love and the rest of my resources.
>
> Good-bye America...you are not the country that I love and I finally realized no matter how much I sacrifice, I can't make you be that country unless you want it."

Nobody teaches you how to be an activist. You get involved, like Cindy, because there's something you care about, and you feel like you've got to give your whole life to the cause because it seems so urgent.

But the world (and any cause) is far bigger and much more resilient than you are. You're quite small, and pretty finite in your energies, and no matter the urgency, if you give everything you've got, I can guarantee you you'll have nothing left, and the need will still be there.

* * *

So what do you do? For yourself and for anyone else you're trying to activate?

You engage your imagination, your sense of fun/hope/ creativity/possibility. You learn as much as you can about the problem, but still try and keep the right kind of ignorance – you keep away from the knowledge that what has to be done is impossible.

As Milo, the main character in The Phantom Tollbooth is told at the end of his unlikely journey:

> "There was one very important thing about your quest that we couldn't discuss until you returned…It was impossible. Completely impossible. But if we'd told you then, you might not have gone. And as you've

discovered, so many things are possible just as long as you don't know they're impossible."

Because who really knows what's possible? History is chock full of people – known and unknown - doing totally impossible things. Revolutionary, audacious, transformational – and true. It's true that a slave ship captain woke up one day, realized that there were people in the hold of his ship, and turned the boat around. He took them all home. And then he wrote the hymn Amazing Grace.

It's true that an Indian lawyer from South Africa peacefully freed India from colonial British rule (that would be Gandhi). It's true that Wangari Matthai won the Nobel prize for planting trees. It's true that a French tightrope walker, Philippe Pettit danced his way across a wire strung between the towers of the World Trade Center (which is not political, but it's totally cool). It's true that a bunch of tree sitters in California saved a Redwood forest from being clearcut. It's true that after 20 years of military rule and two civil wars, Liberia just elected a female president, Ellen Johnson Surleaf.

Now, I don't want you thinking I'm naïve here. It's also true that the world is complex and messy and full of rapacious, dishonest, violent, and/or just plain stupid people who create logjams so choked and insane that it seems impossible to work your way out of them.

So, it's absolutely necessary that you cultivate healthy cynicism, a head for strategy, and a deep understanding of the world and its processes. But at the same time, you still need to figure out how to engage without becoming bitter, despondent, and so cynical that you're paralyzed. Or drunk.

Personally, I think that means you need to become the most effective, creative, and – most importantly – hopeful activists you can [and to be perfectly honest, I don't like being called an activist – I think of what I'm doing as responsible citizenship].

And you can call me – as someone on my mailing list recently did, a Hopium Toker, but I don't believe there's anything wrong with hope. I think hope is vital. Hope is what gets you out of bed in the morning. As the French proverb goes: "Hope is the dream of a soul awake." Or, as Goethe said, "In all things it is better to hope than to despair." And he was German.

Or a more muscled discussion of hope comes from the amazing Howard Zinn, who says:

"To be hopeful in bad times is not just foolishly romantic. It is based on the fact that human history is a history not only of cruelty, but also of compassion, sacrifice, courage, kindness. What we choose to emphasize in this complex history will determine our lives. If we see only the worst, it destroys our capacity to do something. If we remember

those times and places - and there are so many - where
people have behaved magnificently, this gives us the
energy to act, and at least the possibility of sending this
spinning top of a world in a different direction."

* * *

So what cultivates hope? Art, for one. You tell engaging,
inspiring, entertaining stories. You create beautiful,
disturbing, thought-provoking images. You speak the truth of
the world as it is, and then the truth of the world as you want
it to be. Or like I saw the boys do in U23D, you rock peoples'
hearts to a totally different vibrational level. Really, whatever
it takes.

Artists can be the living soul of a culture. Though that idea
can provoke an interesting debate when artists actually start
participating in some aspect of the political process. Like
when movie starts get involved in a cause, the public reaction
often runs along the lines of what do a bunch of dumb actors
know?

While, as an actor myself, this normally infuriates me, I will
allow for making fun of Harrison Ford waxing his chest hair
to demonstrate the pain of tropical deforestation. That was
just silly.

But really, if artists are just dumb and harmless, then why,
when fascism strikes, are we first up against the wall? Why

were so many actors and writers and musicians and painters vilified by the House on Unamerican Activities Committee? Why was folk singer Victor Jara murdered during the 1973 military coup in Chile? Why did Hitler ban van Gogh, Chagall, and Picasso?

The truth is, we're not harmless, and we're not dumb. As Susan Sarandon said, "People should fear art, film, and theatre. This is where ideas happen. This is where somebody goes into a dark room and starts to watch something and their perspective can be completely questioned...the very seeds of activism are empathy and imagination." In other words, we're potent and powerful and dangerous in a wonderful, world-changing way.

It's something I became convinced of following my experience as Co-Founder of the Lysistrata Project. In early 2003, right before the US attacked Iraq, my friend Sharron Bower and I organized over 1000 simultaneous readings of the ancient Greek anti-war comedy Lysistrata in 59 countries and all 50 US states, on 6 continents.

Lysistrata, by the way, tells the story of the women of Greece ending a war by denying sex to their husbands until the men quit fighting. It's a tactic which has also been used in the real world to great effect, and the mere idea of a sex strike tends to freak out anyone suffering from what I call "Old White Man Syndrome."

The act of reading a play as a protest was important, in that it gave people who were disinclined to march in the streets or write letters to the editor or call their congressperson a means of expressing themselves in a way which felt both pointed and playful, but still entirely non-confrontational. Lysistrata Project participants also felt their voice multiplied exponentially by the thousands of other people doing exactly the same thing at exactly the same time. And, it was fun. As our director in NY put it, "Nobody can resist an ancient Greek dick joke."

* * *

Now, in a recent edition of Yes Magazine, the editors posed the question: "What happens when we throw off the invisible chains that keep us from realizing the world we want—when we, as they say in the global south, decolonize our minds?" That's a wonderful question, but we've also got to consider exactly how that happens. How do we learn to see the invisible chains, rattle them, throw them off, and then how do we know what kind of a world it is that we want?

Here, I think, is the greatest purview of the artist. And it happens on a couple different levels. Art shows us the world as it is, allows us to see ourselves, our whole selves, in infinite shades of dark and light. Art reflects ourselves back to us in an intense, highly concentrated, extremely potent, and sneakily digestible form. Often, we relate to what we're seeing and hearing in a work of art long before we recognize our actual selves reflected back. We get surreptitiously trapped in a vision of truth. And once we see, it's very difficult to un-see. It's hard to walk away unchanged.

Beyond that, art allows us to imagine the world as it could be. It's vital to be able to do that, to give a hopeful, inspired vision to move towards, rather than just a raging, dark fear from which to run.

That's all pretty heady, so let me give you a concrete example, in the form of Edi Rama, Mayor of Tirana, Albania. After the fall of Albania's super-insane Communist regime, Tirana was destroyed in civil unrest, the people ruined financially in pyramid schemes. The place was a bombed-out disaster zone. Barely habitable. Edi Rama, who happened also to be a painter, took a look at his broken, hopeless, beloved metropolis, and what did he do?

He started painting blocks of color on the sides of buildings. Primary colors. Like creating a city-sized Mondrian. And it started to change things. He said that the colors weren't dress, they were organs. And they changed the conversations in the street and at the cafes. Changed the level of responsibility people felt about their home. Changed them from victims into...something else.

He said, "To go from a city of destiny to a city of choice is, in itself, a kind of utopia." Edi Rama, in an act of faith, bound by a covenant of love for his city, hit a home run miracle of hope with color.

And there's another important piece of information. The best reason to do the work you're doing is to do it for love. You'll be angry, you'll be sad, you'll be scared. Those things will often get you going. But the long term motivation ultimately has to be love because it's the one thing which won't burn you out, and which never runs out. It's the ultimate in renewable fuel.

* * *

Speaking of fuel, I bet you're wondering about the muffins. Well, when Virginia Fisher first called and asked if I'd come do this talk, I told her I'd do anything, including making you guys muffins. Because I'd just discovered this great banana muffin recipe and I was dying to share it with someone.

That's another part about not burning out. It's about taking time to nurture and nourish yourselves and each other. You can't take care anyone else – at least not for long – if you don't take care of yourself. And you can't take care of others if you don't see yourself in them. If you don't believe with all your heart that they'd love your favorite muffins as much as you do. Banana or wheat allergies aside.

You all know, deep in your soul, that we are all the same, that there is no fundamental difference between you and a Kung bushman or a Chinese factory worker or a Romanian orphan or a Saudi oil magnate or a Berkeley hippie or a movie star who thinks a public chest wax is a high form of political protest.

It's so easy to forget. So easy to vilify someone who has become, for whatever reason, The Other. So easy to allow ourselves to think that somehow, just because a bad thing happened to someone "other" than you, in another part of the world, that their pain is not as great. Or that someone "other" than you who has done something you deem horrible is somehow less human. Less deserving of compassion. But it's not true. Nobody starts out wanting to hurt other people, wanting to rape and kill, wanting to blow up the world. They get to that place from overwhelming despair, crushing poverty, lack of education, extreme ideology, lack of hope.

I don't even think anyone starts out wanting to be, say, an oil executive raking in 10 billion in quarterly profits while most people can barely afford to drive to work or a bank executive who gets millions in bonuses while his industry crumbles around his ankles and thousands of people go bankrupt. I think something happens along the way: a calcification of compassion and an absorption idea that the acquisition of wealth is, somehow, the noblest effort of all.

That doesn't mean you don't want a great life for yourself. Of course you do. You want some combination of love and peace and satisfaction and accomplishment and good friends and chocolate and mountains and football and yoga and sex and TIVO...

But at the same time, you have got to keep your conscience open and ask yourself if anyone is suffering as a result of your actions, as a result of you getting what you want? Are you gaining success or joy or designer jeans or cool toys at someone else's direct expense? Or at the world's expense?

If you are (and most of us are, because that's the way the current system works), then it's a problematic bargain to make – and it exacts a cost on all of us. It engenders a kind of chronic, low grade fear that at some point, we might find ourselves on the wrong side of the equation.

And when you're living in fear, you're in a perpetual state of fight or flight. You're operating from your brain stem, your lizard brain, and when you're in Lizard Brain Mode, you end up making fear-based, short-term choices, which you might not ordinarily make if you were operating from your higher, more mature self. Like electing a lizard president. No offense to lizards.

So, you have got to keep your mind sharp. Your critical faculties polished and tuned. And most importantly, tuned upon yourself.

You've got to ask yourself: What am I doing to alleviate suffering and to support the healthy continuation of all life on the planet? Are you a citizen of – to be extreme about it – are you a citizen of your ego or are you a citizen of the world? Are you driven by love or fear?

And I know that most people are deeply uncomfortable with even considering, much less speaking up about their fears and their passions. But quite honestly, I say unto you: fuck it.

The ice caps are melting and the number of dead zones in the oceans are increasing and 2.7 billion people in the world live on less than $2/day and animals are going extinct at a rate we haven't seen in 65 million years and we're just getting through eight years of an administration which will go down in history as one of the most criminally rapacious, amoral, and self-serving the country has ever seen, and who knows what we could be heading into. We're really long past time to worry about embarrassing ourselves in front of our peers.

But scary as this time is, also know this: as fast as things seem to be falling apart, exponential growth works both ways. We can move from living deeply unsustainable lives to living in harmony with the planet and each other with blinding swiftness. And the faster we choose sustainability, in all its forms, the sooner it happens. As sustainability pioneer Alan AtKisson says,

> "The real basis for hope lines in our willingness to take on this challenge – this responsibility – as one of the central guiding principles in our lives."

And one last thing to remember: You might fail. You might fail at the first try and the 10th and the 100th. You might fail at saving the very thing you love most in the world. But don't stop trying. Howard Zinn says social movements fail a lot before they succeed.

Or I think all the time about that moment at the end of The Two Towers when the Nazgul are attacking Osgiliath, and Sam says to Frodo that there's still some good in the world, and it's worth fighting for. Or like they say in Galaxy Quest, "Never give up, never surrender."

So find out what you love – figure out how to serve – and go for it with all the magic and determination in your heart. Support each other. Have hope. Be revolutionarily creative. And enjoy the muffins.

The Vermont Guide to Global Living
Keynote address for the Vermont Climate Collaborative

Before I get going, I just have a quick question: does anyone here speak German?

I ask because I keep having this...*experience*. Maybe some of you have had it. Where you're doing the work that you do to try to help heal the world, and you're being pretty on-task and focused about it. But then suddenly any distraction or denial you've been hiding behind falls away, and you realize that climate change is really, really real. You're not watching a movie. All these gigantic unravellings are *happening*, much faster than anyone predicted, and it's absolutely chilling. Like ice water in your veins. Anyone ever feel that? If not, why not? What's wrong with you?

So, the phrase I've been using to describe that sock-in-the-gut (and pardon my language, but this is psycho-spiritual terminology here) is a holy fucking shit moment.

The thing is, I've been doing a lot of public speaking lately, and I can't be that overtly Anglo-Saxon everywhere. And I figure if the Germans have a word like *schadenfreude*, happiness at the misfortune of others, they must have a word for when the piano of reality falls on your head from a very great height.

Anyway, hi. Nice to see you all again. And please don't be worried by that little title I gave myself. I don't actually know what a Creative Roustabout and Climate Culture Jammer is. It's just that I don't have anything resembling a normal job, and I can't claim to being a recognizable climate professional. So, when Brian asked for an identifying descriptor, I had to come up with something that would at least confuse you enough to get your attention.

You know, when Brian invited me to speak today, he fell into a long tradition of people calling and saying, "Hi. We'd like you to come talk to us. Can you do something… inspiring?" Every time that happens, I can't help but wonder, *Exactly what would you like me to inspire people to do?*

I asked Brian, but he was a little fuzzy on the specifics. I think he didn't want to get in trouble with Secretary Wood, who gave no more instruction than, and I quote, "Hey! Get that performance artist!" Maybe he thought I'd coat myself with carbon and do an interpretive dance of rising ocean levels and excessive coral bleaching. Which would inspire...what I'm not sure. Maybe inspire you to quit coming to these meetings.

So, I called my friend Jen to brainstorm some ideas and the first thing out of her mouth was, "Oh my god. You're going to make everyone get naked aren't you?"

I hadn't planned on it. But then I did a Facebook poll, and 603 of my friends agree that Jonathan Wood is hot. So maybe it's not such a bad idea...

But no, I'm not going to make you get naked. Though I might ask you shed your preconceived ideas of how the work of the Collaborative is supposed to go.

* * *

But, first, a question. This big document I'm holding is, as you know, is the report from the Governor's Commission on Climate Change. Now be honest. How many of you have read it?

It's pretty good, right? As far as I can tell (not being a recognizable climate professional), it's a thorough piece of work. A lot of deep thinking, great care, and sound reasoning went into its creation. And from asking people who *are* recognizable climate professionals, the recommendations it puts forth are solid and *would* lead to the massive reductions in CO2 emissions that we're looking for.

Now, in spite of all this great work, I can see that you Collaborativos and Collaborativistas are up against a few challenges. For one, while this report is a great descriptor of Vermont's emissions profile, and the recommendations are right on the mark, that's all they are. Recommendations. They're not a detailed action plan for *how* to go about achieving those reductions. Which means you're having to make a bunch of it up as you go along. And that can be a little problematic when you're already up to your eyeballs with your own jobs and lives.

Also, as a work of non-fiction, I have to say that it's pretty...um...dry. If I get excited after 5 pages, it's not because I'm fired up and inspired to get out there and save the world, it's because I actually understood what I just read.

Now you might say, "But Kathy, this wasn't meant for you. You're not a recognizable climate professional. You're not an *expert*. You haven't even learned the secret handshake!"

But I'll contend that in fact this document *was* meant for me (and by me, I mean *any* interested civilian). Partly because it's my future which is at stake, and I want a hand in making sure it's a good one. Also if we, as a state (or a civilization) are going to survive - and thrive - in the face of global climate catastrophe, then we need all hands on deck. Nobody can - or should - be left out of the process, and that process needs to be as accessible as possible.

Another challenge is that the report leaves out two significant issues. One is our current "economic contraction," which happened after the report was written, and diverts a lot of people from the less in-your-face problem of climate change. It also puts all kinds of dents in funding and revenue streams, not to mention injecting the political process with a massive dose of what is technically known as The Crazies.

The other missing piece is peak oil - which we're hitting just about now. Most of you are probably conversant on peak oil, so I'm not going to get into a whole treatise about it, but a couple quick facts for common ground: For every 4 barrels of oil consumed, we discover 1. Of the 98 oil producing nations, 65 have past their peak of production.

I just read that the German army is completely freaking out about this. So is ours. And understandably so.

I mean, the deal-with-it clock for climate change is already ticking double-time, and now add the fact that we in the developed world have an economic system - really, an entire way of life - which is predicated upon a cheap, abundant, and endless supply of fossil fuels.

While we're trying to get off them as quickly as possible and turn to renewables, not only are we moving too slowly, but you can't do a 1:1 replacement. A single liter of oil contains the energetic equivalent of about 5 weeks of hard manual labor. It gives you an energy return that has never been, and cannot be matched by any other source.

That doesn't even take into account all the stuff we *make* out of oil.

But here we are with our settlements, business models, and transportation plans all built on the assumption that we'll have oil in perpetuity, and we've directly linked our economic success to how much oil-drenched stuff we consume.

Somehow we figured sure, we'll reduce carbon emissions as fast as possible, but we'll still have an infinite supply of resources to help us do it. And that's rapidly becoming not the case.

You know, we think of the span of recent history as an oil age, but from a geologic perspective, it's just an interval.   A moment. A breath. But it's a breath during which we have become extremely, profoundly, and thoroughly vulnerable.

* * *

So what are you going to do, you who have been charged with reducing Vermont's carbon emissions as fast as possible?

Well, you *think* you've been charged with that. But given the deep realities of climate change and peak oil, we're not just talking about reduction, mitigation, or adaptation. We're not just talking about changes in policy. We're talking wholesale economic, cultural, behavioral, and spiritual transformation. We're talking about your role as impassioned agents in a planetary extreme makeover so epic that scientists are saying we're leaving holocene and entering the anthropocene - an entirely new geologic era!

And who has the time for *that*?

Well, actually, given that I don't have a real job, I do. So, let's pretend, for the next few minutes, that you have put me in charge. Made me your Climate Tzarina. Or Goddess of the Anthropocene.

So, as Goddess of the Anthropocene, *now* I'm going to make you get naked. Metaphorically speaking. This is when you drop your expectational trou around what you think the Collaborative should be - or is supposed to be - doing.

Because it seems to me that if the Collaborative is mostly comprised of already overloaded folks from UVM and ANR, and you're divided into just four small working groups, then you're creating much more labor and a far greater burden of responsibility than need be borne on your slight but mighty shoulders. It's hardly the most efficient use of your time, or the quickest way to achieve maximum results.

Fortunately, you're not alone. As Alan mentioned, there's a huge community of people out there with vision and vibrancy and enormous amounts of creativity all chomping at the bit to DO SOMETHING. And they are - they're doing a lot.

But what hasn't happened yet is they haven't been brought together into a cohesive whole. They haven't been brought together into a movement, and a movement which has clarity of vision. Because really, what are we all working towards?

And I know we say we're all working to cut our carbon emissions, but that's hardly, to be blunt, sexy.

Ultimately, this isn't about changing our lives as carbon *emitters*, it's about changing them as carbon-based life forms. It's about re-examining and re-creating the very fabric of our existence. Because all of us here have been living a certain kind of life. It's a life in which we know that in spite of all the fun we've had driving and flying and eating beef and starfruit and playing with our Wiis, most of our actions are inherently unsustainable - or worse, truly destructive. And that chips away at even the hardiest soul.

Every ignition key turned, every bit of plastic used once and tossed away, every forest cleared, every giant home built in its place and filled with food and objects which have been grown, mined, and made by anonymous hands from thousands of miles away...it's all a wearing-down not only of our *capacity* to survive, but of our faith in our *ability* to survive.

What do we want? We want lives of peace and meaning and accomplishment and community and love. We want the knowledge that we're not always having to second-guess or flat-out deny the consequences of our behavior.

We want deep integrity and we want genuine hope. We want the answer to a very big question, which is: For all those aspects of life that this community needs in order to sustain itself and thrive, how do we significantly increase resilience (to mitigate the effects of Peak Oil) and drastically reduce carbon emissions (to mitigate the effects of Climate Change)?

* * *

So, where do we look for the answer? For my money, we can turn to another large white book.

This is The Transition Handbook. And honestly, no disrespect meant, but it's a much easier read than the commission's report.

For those of you who don't know about Transition Towns, it's a viral, open-sourced, self-organizing, solutions-focused, non-dogmatic, highly-inclusive methodology for answering that Very Big Question.

Inspired by ecology, systems theory, and permaculture, the transition town model was developed in a little English town called Totnes. I've been there. It's like Montpelier - only instead of a state house, they've got a castle.

Transition Towns were started a few years ago by a guy named Rob Hopkins. Rob and a group of friends took a hard look at climate change and peak oil, and decided to help

Totnes begin the process of what they call "powering down." Powering down means relocalizing food and energy production, working to transform fossil-fueled behaviors, and increasing resilience - which means the community's capacity to absorb and respond to systemic shocks caused by climate change or disruptions in fuel availability, economy, or political systems.

It's a fantastic methodology, and has a lot to do with tapping into the inherent wisdom of a community, and the belief that ordinary people (when they're not being fearmongered into a frothy frenzy) have tremendous knowledge and powerful creative problem-solving capacities.

Transition begins with awareness-raising and education at the local level, and then expands into a series of open conversations all asking the survive/thrive question.

Then they develop theme-based working groups - everything from agriculture to energy to reskilling to local economy. They even have a heart and soul group, recognizing the emotional and spiritual challenge of living in These, Our Troubled Times.

Eventually, they come up with what's called an Energy Descent Action Plan, which is a community-developed roadmap for how they're going to work their way through this process. And then they carry it out.

This is the Energy Descent Action Plan for Totnes. It's comprehensive, well-written, and even though it's unflinching about the big scary stuff, it definitely passes the bedside table test. By that I mean if you read it before you go to bed, it'll give you good dreams, rather than nightmares.

There are over 300 Transition initiatives around the world, and we could easily launch one in Vermont. Again, as Alan mentioned, there's already so much in place to help it get rolling. We've got nearly 2 dozen active local transition groups and almost 100 town energy committees. Vermont Interfaith Power and Light has over 50 participating congregations, and we've got dozens of schools, universities, libraries, and museums committed to climate-based education. There are countless growers, gardeners, permaculture groups, farmer's markets, restaurants, co-ops, and composters all helping build our local food economy.

We're the seat of the activist group 350.org, which as you know is about to do another global day of action on October 10. We hosted the first US conferences on Gross National Happiness and slow money, and we have people experimenting with microlending and developing local currencies. We've got volunteer groups doing neighborhood home energy assessments and teaching everything from bike repair and scything to building earth ovens, earth homes, root cellars, and rain barrels. And *everyone* I know seems to have their own personal chicken.

We're bursting with scientists and consultants and non-profits galore, from well-known groups like VNRC and VPIRG - who's just launched a whole Solar Communities program - to Local Motion and the Good Earth Singers - who are trying to save the planet with song.

Vermont Businesses for Social Responsibility has hundreds of members, many of whom are national leaders in their field. We have artists and writers and actors and musicians and dancers and graphic designers and home crafters. We're so close to what we could become. Or, as Arundhati Roy famously said, "Another world is not only possible, she is on her way. On a quiet day, I can hear her breathing."

* * *

So let's imagine how we might hear that other world's breath just a little more clearly. And I'm not laying out a formal game plan here. There's no single way to do this. I'm just letting my mind wander into the realm of possibility. So let your naked mind wander along with me, and get your naked mind toes a little dirty. Dream big.

First let's imagine bringing representatives from all those groups together for a Statewide Convergence of All Beings. I'd also add folks from labor and health care and Refugee Resettlement, since that's something we're going to have to deal with more and more. Also state agencies and selectboardspeople and members of the legislature and the national delegation. We'll need energy producers - both new school and old - and builders and bankers and the press and the Vermont League of Cities and Towns and the Arts and Humanities councils, and the Vermont Community Foundation. Since money is always nice.

Oh. And the Governor. And probably a really good therapist.

Now, I don't know where we'd meet, because we're up to about 14,000 people. But fortunately, in my mind, there's room for everyone.

First off, we'd agree that, like the Blues Brothers, we're on a Mission From God. Or Goddess, since you've put me in charge. Our goal is to help Vermont make the swiftest, smoothest, most proactive, and participatory transition to a post-carbon life. And to serve as a replicable model for the rest of the country.

We start with a statewide education program designed to bring everyone up to speed on the issues. Maybe we tie it in to the Vermont Humanities Council's Vermont Reads program, and get everyone both reading and doing the CO2 reduction program in *The Low Carbon Diet*. This is the book that Interfaith Power and Light's eco-teams have been using to great success.

Imagine every town in Vermont and all the cable access channels screening films like *Wake Up, Freak Out, Then Get A Grip, No Impact Man,* and *The Power of Community.*

Imagine libraries and coffee shops and churches and grange halls taking on the formal role of Climate Cafe, a place where people can gather to talk and process and educate themselves and each other. The climate cafes can be where idea-generating conversations happen, and where people form local working groups and plan small-scale projects.

Imagine volunteers all over the state becoming trained Climate Ambassadors - people who wear a big Climate Ambassador button and are willing to chat up folks on the street, share information, and collect ideas which can be transmitted back to the state-level leadership.

Imagine that state-level leadership, made of a diverse spread of community representatives, taking all this input, building on the commission's report, and developing Vermont's Energy Descent Action Plan, something which communicates back to Vermonters their vision of where we're headed, lays out a detailed roadmap for how we're going to get there, and offers solid metrics of progress so that we can easily keep track of how we're doing.

Imagine artists creating all kinds of installations and performances which reflect the transformation being undertaken, and help keep the collective vision at the forefront of everyone's mind. Imagine simultaneous statewide parties celebrating the goals we achieve along the way.

Also, I have an idea for getting massive international attention by staging a press conference where we formally invite Santa Claus to relocate to Vermont now that the North Pole is melting.

* * *

And what will we actually *do* as we power down? We'll follow the meatiest of the commission's recommendations. We'll localize food and energy production. We'll solve the problem of how to get people out of their cars and develop rural public transportation networks. We'll honor the tradition of the independent town and bring living, work, and educational space back to the center of our communities. We'll keep our forests intact and our landfills empty.

We'll also make room for people from the broken and vanished places of the world, and welcome their contributions, their wisdom, and their capacity for survival. We'll listen to each other, entertain each other, sing and dance and cook and cry with each other, and support each other as the shape of our lives cannot help but change.

We've been so fortunate to have lived through this petroleum interval. It's brought us enormous adventure and freedom and unprecedented novelty and wealth. It's been a fantastic party. And I don't think anybody ever intended to trash the planet along the way.

But we have, and that's enough to crack your heart.

Know, though, that when your heart cracks, you can either die of grief, duct tape it together and solider on, or you can let all those cracks and open spaces get filled up by love. It's like cracks in cement. Water gets in there, and things start to grow. Life happens in those cracks. The same is true for us, and it's an amazing thing to see.

And lumpy and syncopated as the process is, it's happening. Everywhere around the world, people are startled and scared by the truth that we're just a bunch of critters living on one tiny, miraculous rock in space and we have absolutely nowhere else to go.

We're realizing how much we love our little rock, and we're deciding that it's worth being unstintingly selfless and creative and courageous in order to save it. And ourselves.

So, you can go ahead and put your mental clothes back on now. But do it slowly, and don't tie anything too tight. Have faith. Be brave. Show your love. And take time to listen to the breath, the call, the song of that other world. Because she is on her way. She is on her way. She is on her way. And your hands can open the door.

Care Like No-One's Watching

Keynote address for the
Howard Center for Human Services Annual Fundraiser

They arrived in the middle of the night. Arlene wasn't asleep.
She might have been, but then again, maybe not. Sleep's been
like Burlington's weather these days – erratic and cold.
Inescapably cold.

Anyway, cold and late as it was, she wasn't asleep. She was
knitting.

What with the price of heat shooting up like the dickens,
Arlene has taken the art of layering to a whole new level.

She doesn't mind the bulk, but the act of putting on undershirt
after undershirt after shirt after shirt after sweater after
sweater after fleece after a final wrap in Tyvek was just getting
to be a little bit much.

So she's spent most of the last few weeks going to Goodwill,
picking ratty old sweaters out of the dollar bin, unraveling
them, and re-knitting them into a garment of Biblical
proportions. Joseph's coat of many colors transformed into a
multi-hued, triple-thick union suit. That much wool weighs a
lot, so the whole thing is a little baggy. The crotch tends to
slide down around her knees. But she just holds it up with
Owen's old tool belt. The contractor kind with a buckle *and*

suspenders, and multiple compartments dangling around the equator of her waist. Makes her feel like freakin' Batman.

She's got compartments for snacks, pills, the phone (not too many folks calling these days, but at least she doesn't have to go searching for it). Even her dumb little yellow cat Twinkie rides around in the big nail pouch sometimes. She's got the hammer sling rigged for her knitting needles and a special pocket for yarn. The day it dropped below zero, she knit herself fingerless mittens and attached them to the sleeves of the union suit without even taking it off.

She doesn't wear this thing in public, mind you. She's got a little pride left. And plus, Owen, even if he was watching her from the farthest reaches of Hell, would laugh himself silly. But it's just the thing for lounging around at home. If you could call wondering what the heck she's going to do with her worn-down, gimpy old self "lounging."

The night they arrived, she was in the middle of making a new cap with extra-large earflaps when heard a commotion at the front door. Peeking out the window, she saw a crowd of people – looks like even a few kids – scootching their way into the building. Hard to tell, exactly, given the dark and the fact that they're all bundled up like a family of Goodyear tire people.

Arlene's pretty sure none of her neighbors would be having a party in the dead hollow of of a Tuesday night, so she limps out to the landing to see what's what and who's who. "Hey there!" she calls out. Seven or eight faces look up, and to her great surprise, a bunch of them are as dark as the night they came in from. Darker than she's ever seen in her life.

"Hello!" responds a…a…oh, how do you say it these days? She's a not-dark woman. Ok, ok, she's white. "I'm Jill. We're here helping with this… This is a family from Somalia. Some of the family, at least. Do you know about Somalia? It's a country in… Oh, well, we don't have time for that right now. But anyway, they just got off the plane, and now they're going to be living here! They're your new neighbors!"

"Oh," says Arlene. "Hey there."

Seven or eight pairs of eyes stare back at her. The lowest-lying eyes, giant, dark, and set deep in the head of a kid about 5 or so, get very, very wide. The mouth below the eyes lets out a little, "Eeeep!" An adult hand moves quickly over the kid's mouth. There is a long pause.

"Ok then," says Arlene. And she hobbles back into her apartment, a little confused by the family's response.

That is, she's confused until she turns around and catches a glimpse of herself in the mirror by the front door. There she is, a bulbous, baggy, multicolored monster with dangling pouches, long needles, and wide red suspenders.

Arlene grunts. "Hm. Welcome to freakin' America!"

* * *

Those are the beginning paragraphs of a short story called *The Gifty Part of the Year,* which I wrote for Vermont Stage Company's annual production of *Winter Tales,* which is an ecumenically-oriented holiday show full of stories and songs celebrating the winter season and the various and sundry religious, spiritual, and community-oriented festivities contained therein.

How's that for a diplomatic and artfully non-partisan description? While still being just ever-so-slightly self-promoting?

Actually, I wouldn't have brought up the story, Winter Tales, or Vermont Stage Company at all if it hadn't been for the fact that it was this very piece which prompted the folks at Howard Center to ask me to come speak at this event (an invitation for which I'm deeply grateful because these guys are amazing). They felt the story reflected the spirit and purpose of Howard Center – helping people who can't make it on their own – and that all the characters, from Arlene the knitter to the transplanted Sudanese family whom she surreptitiously adopts, are people who could easily have real-life counterparts within the Howard Center community.

Now the tricky part was that when I sat down with Gail Rosenberg to talk about how this evening would go, she basically said to me, "So we'd love it if you'd read that *Gifty* story, and also talk about Howard Center and all our programs, and also of course subtly encourage people to donate lots of money, but not *too* much because you're also welcome to talk about what you do at Vermont Stage Company and I know you guys need donations, too, and then oh, also, I know you haven't actually *written* this talk – you probably haven't even thought about it yet – but we've got an early deadline at the printer's so can you also come up with a title for your speech and a quote we can include in the program and the invitation? Oh, and also, you're going last and it's going to be a long evening, so can you keep your remarks to about 15 minutes max?"

"Sure!" I said. "No problem!"

By the way, Gail Rosenberg is a woman who absolutely LOVES her job, LOVES Howard Center (rightly so), and you should all spend time in her presence just to soak up the vibes from someone who emanates joy and satisfaction and hope and utterly open-hearted enthusiasm. We should all be so lucky.

So, anyway, "Sure!" I said. "No problem!" But I'm actually not going to do any of what she asked for. At least not yet.

* * *

First, I want to tell you about something else. I recently attended Vermont Businesses for Social Responsibility's annual conference. Did any of you go? It's a great event to go to when you want to find yourself in the presence of smart, innovative, ethical, pragmatically idealistic business leaders who care about making the world a better place and actually know how to make it happen.

The challenge for me, though, was that the keynote speaker was a Pulitzer Prize-winning journalist who has spent years investigating and uncovering the horribly unjust ways in which the government spends the public's money. This, of course, is totally righteous work.

But he spent his *entire* speech talking about how this country is dominated by a fiscal oligarchy which has passed numerous laws designed to take from the poor to give to the rich in all manner of nefarious ways. How when you get sick, your taxes get raised in order to fund tax cuts for the super-rich. How we reward companies for moving their assets offshore. How it's impossible to get a meeting with one's Congressional representative because they're completely monopolized by lobbyists. It was just 45 minutes of Unremitting Gloom.

When he was done, a woman stood up and said, "Ok, you've just completely depressed all of us. So what do we do?" And he replied, "Bug your Senators."

Which was, I thought, a totally pathetic answer.

So, I went up to him afterwards and said, "What's your goal in talking to a group like this?" And he said, "To make people aware of what's going on." And I said, "Well, you're the expert here, do you have a comprehensive strategy for addressing the problem?" Because I figured he'd just had a crowd of high-minded people right in his lap who'd totally be his Army of Righteousness if he'd presented them with a serious plan – or even just a couple good ideas. His response? "Read my book." He also made a point of letting me know that the reviews had been very, very good.

I bring this up because it's exactly the kind of information we hear about in the news all the time. And really, we hear about it in *all* the news – from FOX to Truthout, from NPR to The National Review, from Democracy Now to The Wall Street Journal – it all seems to be some version of the narrative about who's being screwed or who's doing the screwing or how to make sure you're the screw-er and not the screw-ee. And it can really want to make you take to your bed with a Teddy Bear and a big mug of Adult Ovaltine. It can make you want to give up or check out or focus on what you can get for you and yours and not worry about the rest of the picture, because, Wake Up And Smell The Coffee Money Makes The World Go Round People In Power Will Do Anything To Stay In Power We're All Going To Hell In A Handbasket and Things Just Don't Ever Change.

And admittedly, that's a true narrative. Or at least a true-ish narrative. But it's not the whole truth. It's not the complete story of what's going on in the world from day to day. It's charismatic and shocking and gigantic and important and definitely gets the most noise and ink and attention. But it's not the whole truth. And we know that, in part, thanks to Howard Center.

Howard Center embodies different kind of truth. In fact it's an antidote to that Other Truth. It's the truth that yes, there is a world of fiscal currency – money and power and might and finance and all that stuff. But there's also a whole world of social currency, a world of power-under rather than power-over, which involves investing time and energy and resources in your community, investing in the homeless, the sick, the troubled, the lost, investing in the people who need the most help, and providing the tools and resources they need to make their lives functional and whole.

And the people of Howard Center know that those kind of investments pay unimaginable – and often unmeasurable – dividends: moral dividends, psychological dividends, cultural dividends. They know that in the world of social currency, it's almost impossible to set up a ponzi scheme or bundle risk or be stuck with a heap of toxic assets.

Of course, they DO still need the regular kind of currency to do their work, which – let us not forget – is what this whole evening is about. Hint hint.

* * *

You know, I was in the little town of Vergennes, Vermont last week, and I met a guy named Kevin Dann who's on a peace walk from Montreal to NYC as his way of commemorating the Lake Champlain Quadrecentennial. He talked about the challenge of doing this whole big walk and meeting all these incredible peace-makers along the way, but not knowing if anyone was watching, not knowing if he's having any kind of real impact. The troubles of the world all seem so huge to him.

He said in particular he can't stop thinking about how were torturing Native Americans back when Champlain came to the region, and we were torturing people in the Philippines 100 years ago and we're still torturing people today, and nobody's talking about it, he can't even get his lefty peace-making friends to talk about it, and how will it ever stop. He was walking because he was compelled to, because he HAD to, but deep down he wondered: Is anyone *really* paying attention? Can I make any kind of difference at all?

I completely understood what he meant. Not many people have the luxury of knowing that their work really and truly makes a difference. And I felt particularly bad for him –

partly because I've had those same thoughts about a zillion times, but also because there'd been this big article about him in *7 Days* which I hadn't seen at all and I sure wasn't going to tell him that!

But I also didn't want to leave him hanging. So I repeated an old fable a friend once told me about a Sparrow who hears that the sky is going to fall. And so he lies down on his back and holds his legs up in the air. And the king's soldier comes along and says, "What are you doing little sparrow?" And the Sparrow says, "The sky is going to fall, and I'm holding it up." "With those skinny little legs?" "Well," says the Sparrow, "someone's got to try."

People like Kevin Dann – and the folks at Howard Center – do what they do – those sparrow-like acts of foolish courage, of quiet compassion, or fierce advocacy – not because it's going to work, necessarily. They do them because it's right. They take action because someone has to try and because taking action is what keeps their spirits and their hearts alive.

The cool part is, though, all the stuff that the people at Howard Center do? It DOES work! All the programs they offer and the passionate, committed people who run them DO make a difference. And even better, they know it! They get to see the results of their work in action all the time. And STILL they don't care if anyone is watching – except for tonight when they're asking for your help to pad their little feathered backs and bolster their skinny little legs and support their continued efforts.

The people of Howard Center keep the sky from falling in the lives of many, many individuals and families and they give hope where none existed before. They care where nobody else does. They care, in the words of that beautiful phrase from Matthew, for the least of these our brethren. For the least among us.

Except Howard clients are hardly the least. Especially not to themselves. And the good folks at Howard Center know that, too. They know the deep value of the fragile and the wounded and the lost people of the world, because they know that nobody really thinks of themselves as fragile and wounded and lost. They might need a little bit of help – or a whole lot of help – but that's in service of bringing themselves and their gifts and their skills and their love back out into the light. Out into being a part of life.

And the people of Howard Center aren't doing it just for their clients – who clearly need the help. Nor are they doing it just for themselves – because service is their life's purpose. The people at Howard Center are also doing it for you. Because every act of healing makes us all a little more whole.

You didn't have to be here tonight. You could have ignored the invitation or just sent in a check. But you came. And you don't even have to give any more money. Nobody's really watching, and you already paid for your tickets. If you don't give, the people of Howard Center will still go on doing the good work they do.

If you do give I'm sure you'll get a lovely note of thanks, but it's not like you'll get your name in the paper or win an award.

But that's not why you're here. That's not why you're going to give tonight, and give generously.

You're here and you're giving for two reasons. You're giving because of your enormous gratitude for the great fortune of your life – for finding yourself in the remarkable position of being able to help out in the first place.

And you're giving because you know that by giving, by raising your little limbs in the air, you are helping to hold up someone's sky.

Thank you.

March In

Keynote address for the
Vermont Women's Fund Birthday Bash and Fundraiser

As someone who clomps frequently back and forth over the line between arts and activism – as well as the sacred and the profane – I have to tell you that when Brenda Bisbee first contacted me about doing a little something for this remarkable celebration, I had several simultaneous, conflicting thoughts – mostly because she wasn't too specific in her request.

She basically said, "I'm turning 80 and Emma's turning 30 and we get along great and we're having a big party, so can you create a 15 or so minute piece that's funny and inspiring and about women because it's a benefit for the Women's Fund and suffrage since it's the 90th anniversary. I guess that's all. Oh, but..." her voice got very quiet, "remember these are committed, professional feminists. So you'll have to make it *really* funny."

Thought 1A was: Is that *all*?

Thought 1B was: What am I going to talk about in front of a group of women who already spend their lives on the front lines of social justice? If I tell them that running a non-profit like the Women's Fund is hard but noble work, they're going to exhale, roll their eyes, and give me a giant collective, "Duuuhhh!"

Oh, and let me not omit the fact that Brenda also made a big point of telling me - several times - that there would be people of the male persuasion here tonight. And I see you. Hi Guys! I'm not quite sure why she needed to keep reminding me, or what she feared I might do to alienate or embarrass you fellas. Maybe flip my skirts up over my head, show you the sparkling antenna with which I've adorned my gal parts, and declare, "Check it out! Now it really *does* look like a butterfly!"

I'm not going to do that. So you can all relax. Or be disappointed. Or see me in the bathroom a little later.

So, another Bisbee-inspired thought was: Wow. The 90th anniversary of women's suffrage. Amazing. But where the heck does the word *suffrage* come from? It's not very... *attractive*. Couldn't they come up with something prettier? More stylish? I mean, we are *women* after all! If we're going to have a movement can't we at least make it aesthetically pleasing?

Well, I looked up the etymology of suffrage, and it's from the Latin *suffragium*, meaning vote, political support, and the right to vote. So it's technically accurate, but it's still a horrible word. It sounds like, you know, suffering!

Ok, let's just admit it. Women's Suffrage sounds like a euphemism for menstrual cramps. It sure doesn't sound like something for which you'd want to spend 75 years fighting and getting beaten up and put in jail and spending lots of time in North Dakota like Susan B. Anthony did and going toe to toe with the US Senate...

And speaking of the Senate – it's actually a relief to know that 90 years ago they weren't a much more noble and illustrious legislative body than they are today. In fact, some say the etymology of suffrage comes from *sub* – under – and *fragor* – crash, din, and shouts. Which *totally* sounds like the Senate.

So, I'm sure you all know the suffrage story, but just so we're on the same page here: in 1837 a young teacher named Susan B. Anthony had the audacity to ask for equal pay for women teachers. A year later, in July, 1838, the first women's rights convention was held in Seneca Falls, NY. Nobody ever asks why Seneca Falls of all places, so I did a little research on that as well.

Turns out that in the early years of the Victorian era, Seneca Falls was one of those locales which hosted conventions all the time. Apparently, in checking out potential conference sites, Elizabeth Cady Stanton heard that Seneca Falls was also hosting a simultaneous convention of doctors learning how to do these newfangled vibrator treatments for women's "hysteria," and she thought perhaps it'd be an opportunity to mix a little business with pleasure.

Fortunately the marketing slogan for the convention center was "What happens in Seneca Falls stays in Seneca Falls."

The suffragists learned a lot that weekend. And if you ever wondered how the movement was able to endure until August 26, 1920 when the US Secretary of State signed the Anthony Amendment into law, *that* my friends, is the great unspoken secret of women's history.

Still, it was a long and fraught struggle, and in the end, the biggest roadblock to women achieving the full voting rights of any regular old butt-scratching guy on the street was a bunch of conservative Southerner Senators who were afraid that if women got the vote, they'd pass prohibition, and then gosh darn it, where would the moonshine industry be?

It's always the economy, isn't it? Always. And somehow, no matter how great the injustice du jour – say suffrage, or slavery, or perhaps unaffordable health care – the looming shadow of some *potentially* negative economic consequence somehow seems inevitably worse than what's actually happening right now. No matter how morally degraded the collective conscience is by the great big wrong being perpetrated.

I've been thinking about that a lot lately – how we have this cultural cognitive economic dissonance. Ok, pithy phrase, but you probably have no idea what I'm talking about. Let me back up.

* * *

I had a day recently where I overheard 3 conversations in a row in which someone said, "Corporations control everything, and there's nothing we can do."

The speakers were a businessman, a student, and an activist, and every single time, I thought, "Really? *Everything?* Have you talked to my cat lately?"

These conversations came in the context of talking about how to address climate change, and the point was that the fundamental obstacles to our taking action on climate change are purely economic. And as long as human beings, and more significantly, the kind of human beings we call "corporations" have the capacity to maximize profit, they will, to the detriment of anyone or anything which stands in their way.

And it occurred to me that this must cause all kinds of psycho-spiritual chaos in many of the actual *homo sapien* human beings who work for those corporations.

Because what do we say we value in our personal lives? Love, respect, family, commitment. What do we value in our leaders at a local level? All the deacons and little league coaches and various community pillars? We say we value honesty. Integrity. Fairness.

We even say we value sacrifice – what parents do for their kids or what we say we honor more than anything – military sacrifice. Dying to "preserve our freedoms" or at the very least save the squad.

Of course, we're human. Fallible. We fail at being honest and fair and respectful all the time. But it's the direction towards which the angels of our better natures are always telling us to head.

Except for when it comes to business. You do something immoral, unjust, or even merely unkind, and there's a casual shrug in response. A shrug accompanied by the phrase, "It's just business." *Just* business? Like somehow it stands completely apart from the moral fabric of the rest of our lives. Which may be true, but it must set up a crazy kind of psycho-spiritual disharmony to have two completely different sets of rules governing our existence.

Not to mention the fact that nobody thinks of themselves as the Bad Guy. Everyone is the star – and therefore the heroine or hero – of their own movie. And so even as someone is working to maximize profit, they must also think – or have convinced themselves that they are – doing good on a personal level. Even though from an objective standpoint, it's clear that sometimes something's gotten lost in the shuffle.

* * *

And what does this have to do with suffrage? With women's rights? With all of you and Brenda and Emma and the Women's Fund and whether or not I show you my sparkly antennae?

Well, that brings us to another thought I had when Brenda approached me. Or rather the song which started ringing through my head. *Bread and Roses*. Which was inspired by a 1912 textile workers' strike in Lowell, Massachusetts.

> *As we go marching marching*
> *in the beauty of the day*
> *A million darkened kitchens*
> *A thousand mill lofts grey*
> *Are touched with all the radiance*
> *That a sudden sun discloses*
> *For the people here are singing*
> *Bread and roses bread and roses*

Beautiful. But it's the third verse that really gets me:

> *As we go marching marching*
> *We battle too for men* (so there's another shout-out for the guys)
> *For they are women's children*
> *And we mother them again* (though hopefully not all the time)
> *Our lives shall not be sweated*
> *From birth until life closes*

Hearts starve as well as bodies
Give us bread but give us roses

Hearts starve as well as bodies. Give us bread but give us roses.

I think that's why Brenda called – the collective birthday present she was really after.

Every struggle for justice is hard. Every attempt to change systems and shift paradigms and right wrongs is long and complex and endlessly demanding and overwhelmingly challenging. As Howard Zinn said, social movements fail – and fail a lot – before they succeed. And even success isn't a singular thing. Yes, women got the right to vote, but you all know how much work there's still to be done. It isn't a singular battle, it's a continuous process, with an infinite number of successes and failures along the way.

And no matter what challenges we're facing, no matter how murky the prospects, even in the darkest depths of the struggle, we need roses. We need art and laughter. We need to come together in celebration and nurture those angels of our better nature who are constantly working to keep our humanity intact – despite all the contradictions and dissonances. We need to keep our souls full of wonder and our energy high for the lifetimes of world-tending work needing to be done.

And you'll note that the song doesn't ask for Bread and Rubies. Or Bread and Rolls Royces. Just roses. Grown from the earth, tended by our own hands, and connecting us to the magic of how seed and water and sunlight miraculously transmogrify into heart-exploding beauty.

Art. Music. Poetry. Flowers. Celebration. Community. They're not luxuries. They are the food of our spirit. They are *really* how we preserve our freedoms. They're how we claim the power and agency of our true, individual, homo sapien humanity – whether we're 80 or 30 or anywhere above, below, betwixt or between.

Which leads me to my final thought.

* * *

I remember, when I was in my early 20s, hearing a number of women just a little older than I was say something to the effect of, "I'm 30! And I'm not going to take it anymore!" Like for years they'd felt the obligation to put up with an enormous amount of crap, and they finally decided such crap was no longer required for the advancing of their careers or relationships.

Of course, at 10 years younger, I was still reeling from the reality of just being present in the world. Like my personal declaration was, "I'm 20! And I'm here! Really! Hellooooo!"

And it gets me thinking that perhaps every decade has its own kind of declaration of independence which deserves to be shouted and celebrated. I know for me now, having entered my 40s, I keep having this uncanny sense of finally having a rightful place at the table – or even creating my own damn table – and of being very clear about what I'm good at, and owning it in a very unabashed way. Like, "I'm 42 and I am indeed funny and inspiring – with or without sparkling labial antennae. So deal."

A friend of mine from high school concurred when she said, "for me, my 30s mantra was "I don't have to take this crap." For my 40s, so far, it has been "Regardless of what you think, I am doing the right thing."

In fact, concern (or lack thereof) about what someone else thinks seems to be an ongoing theme for women. A voice teacher of mine recently said, "The best part about being 60 is that you *really* don't care what anyone else thinks." Then she added, "And I'm going to gift that not caring to you now, so you don't have to wait another 20 years for it."

It was one of the best presents I ever got. And Emma, in case you need it, I'll pass that shortcut along to you. In fact, everybody here, guys included, if you have any shred left of caring what anyone else thinks about you...*SHAZAM!* It's gone. Take a breath! What a relief! Go forth and...I don't know...dance badly.

Of course, there are a few more decades I'm not really clear about and hopefully if you catch Brenda later, here at her 80th birthday, she'll drop of few pearls of wisdom and perspective your way.

Really, this is all about marking the stages of growing up, of maturing – something with which I've had a less than enthusiastic relationship. I think I feared that growing up meant ossifying, getting more staid, swearing less, dressing more conservatively, nothing sparkly *anywhere*...

What's been exciting, though, is realizing I was completely wrong about it. Turns out, growing up is about deepening. Using all your experiences to find a richness of understanding, of wisdom, of perspective. It's about mending the dissonances and getting psycho-spiritually fabulous and having sparkles in your soul – something *anyone* can see without getting embarrassed.

It's like in Madeline L'Engle's book *A Wind In The Door* where these little juvenile mouse-creatures called Farandolae are wreaking havoc on the world because all they want to do is zoom around in wild circles. They refuse to deepen, to mature into their adult form, called Farae, which are kind of like trees. They're rooted in one spot. The Farandolae think being a Farae is going to be really boring.

Then, an adult Farae named Senex says, "It is only when we are fully rooted that we are really able to move." Of course the Farandolae think that's a big pile of mouse-creature poo. But Senex, who's gotten kind of cosmic, continues: "Now that I am rooted I am no longer limited by motion. Now I may move anywhere in the universe. I sing with the stars. I dance with the galaxies. I share in the joy – and in the grief."

Now, as you go through your *own* maturation, you may not get to the point of singing with the stars or dancing with the galaxies. But you probably do feel yourself deepening; deepening in your knowledge of who you are, and what you're capable of, but most especially in your capacity to share equally in the joy and the grief. In your capacity for compassion.

And I think that for anyone who aspires to be an agent of change, true, Capital C, Buddha-style compassion is the most valuable tool of all. It gives you patience and perspective and the ability to speak the gentle truth in any situation. It allows you to operate from a place of love and vision, rather than anger and fear. You can be generous because you know that when you're grounded in yourself, you have nothing you can lose.

Compassion enables you to be a maker of change just by your very presence. It makes you a wind in the door. You ruffle the curtains of the status quo just by walking – or marching – in. After all, as the song concludes:

As we go marching marching

We bring the greater days
For the rising of the women
Means the rising of the race
No more the drudge and idler
Ten that toil where one reposes
But a sharing of life's glories
Bread and roses, bread and roses

So march in, all you fabulous, sparkly, emotionally mature, truth-telling, utterly uncontrolled, art-loving, non-crap-taking, rose-growing, grief-and-joy-sharing, compassionate agents of change! March in! March in! March in! March in! March in!

Moving Planet

Opening remarks for the Vermont Moving Planet Rally - part of 350.org's international day of climate action.

Hello Vermont! Welcome to Moving Planet!

This is a day to move move move move move! Move beyond fossil fuels, move beyond business as usual, move beyond denial and doubt and inaction and jump the climate movement to a whole new level of breadth and power.

So, in the spirit of moving beyond fossil fuels, how many of you carpooled here today? How many walked? How many walked from someplace really far away? And can we hear from the cyclists out there?

Thanks for coming, huge thanks to our sponsors: Ben&Jerry's, The Sierra Club, All Earth Renewables, Hunger Mountain Coop, City Market, and Green Energy Times. And super-duper thanks to all the legions of businesses, non-profits, and individuals who made this event happen. This event was organized by a collaborative team of dozens of people from all over the state, and If you had something to do with it - and you know who you are - take a moment to jump up and down and and wave your hands in the air. If you see someone with their hands up, high five em. Or give 'em a big kiss if they're cute. You people are amazing!

Just so you know, today there are over 2000 Moving Planet events in 172 countries around the world.

People from pole to pole have been organizing and painting and building and biking and swimming and stilt-walking and rollerblading and partying (that would be Brazil) for weeks in preparation for this day.

There is a movement happening on this moving planet. And for those of you who have been wondering what a movement looks like, I say just turn your head. Look around you.

You are standing in the middle of a movement.

This event here is a bead in the mala, the rosary, of joyous, powerful, meaningful protests all over the world - protests which are blazing with chutzpah, purpose, and dynamic, devoted action.

And not just this day. For months we've been watching as, in the most unlikely places, the people rise up. They take to the streets. They march and sing and tweet and sit and get hurt and stand strong and share food, and inspire everyone around them. And whether it's for a new government, a new economic system, a new social structure, or a new atmosphere, it's really the same message.

From Egypt to Tunisia to Bahrain, Syria, Lebanon, Morocco, New York, Washington, D.C. - and now Montpelier, Vermont -

people are putting their bodies in the streets to say, "We have damaged each other enough. We have damaged our world enough. And now there must be change. Now there must be justice."

The people of Planet Earth are saying with their bodies in the streets, "We have a vision! We believe we can build a better life for all the creatures who share this gorgeous little celestial orb. We can have clean air, clean water, abundant food, good jobs, healthy forests, and beautiful, cohesive communities. We can live lightly, caringly, gently on this tiny little blue ball floating in the vast emptiness of space. We can care well for our one and only home. We can and we must. We absolutely must. Because there is no Planet B."

The people of the world are saying with their bodies in the streets, "We can bring atmospheric CO2 back down to 350 ppm and repair what has been broken."

And even though it won't be easy, even though it won't be quick, even though we're fighting forces with tiny minds, gigantic greed, and even bigger bank accounts, we believe we can do it. We can win the fight for a healthy home. And we will do it with joy and resolve. We will do it with power and passion. We will do it with dazzling vision and radical pragmatism. We will do it with hearts and smarts.

We will set our goals as high in the sky as we can, and then, like Vermonters have been doing for each other all over the state, we will roll up our sleeves, put on our boots, and turn our shovels to the muck at hand.

The muck at hand. How many of you here were touched by the flooding? How many of you here spent time helping clean up? How many of you saw the wreckage and knew in your bones that the planet we live on now is not the one we were born to? And how many of you know in your bones that when we set out to rebuild, we must rebuild for life on this new planet, a place where the atmosphere is heating up, the oceans are acidifying, the ecosystems are unravelling, the weather is unpredictably rough and the floods and droughts come often? And how many of you, knowing all that, are dedicating your lives to the healing of the world?

You are not alone in your commitment. All over the lawn here, across this state, all over the country, all around the world, you have brothers and sisters whose arms are linked in yours. They are everywhere: from Annapolis to Abidjan, from Berlin to Bangalore, from Lima to Lagos, they gather together with joy and resolve. They stand by your side. And they all shout the same number. 350. 350. 350. 350. 350...

So, are you ready for some great speakers? Good. Cuz we've got 'em. And we picked these people for a reason.

Vermont is about to put forth a comprehensive 20-year energy plan. Governor Shumlin, who'll be here later today, and his administration - they all have a deep understanding of the urgent need to take action on climate change, and we commend them for the hard work they're doing. But they also need our help. Strong ideas and solid intentions too easily get watered down in the harsh realities of the political process. And we are here to make sure that doesn't happen.

We are here to say it's great that you want clean energy, but it has to be clean energy for all. And not only that, but we need 100% clean energy for all. Not 50, not 60, not 80, not even 90%. 100% clean energy for all! And soon!

We are here to say these are serious times, the clock is ticking, and the hour is so late that really, we get one shot at this! One! So why go for anything less than exactly what has to be done? No matter how hard. No matter how radical. No matter how politically problematic it seems.

We are here to say it's wonderful that you want healthy, local food, but it has to be healthy local food for all. Green transport, intact forests, energy efficient buildings, green jobs - they have to be for all. All Vermonters. Because this is what justice looks like. And we want to be able to face our children and grandchildren and say that we did everything we possibly could for justice.

We are here to say that these things must be achieved as fast as possible, with bold, visionary, transformative solutions. We are here to say that the scale of the response has got to equal the scope of the problem. Because the problem is huge. The problem is beyond huge. The problem is utterly unprecedented.

But so is the size of our hearts. So is the depth of our commitment. So is the will of the people of Vermont.

We are are a small state with a very large sense of purpose. We've got a governor and a congressional delegation who are all climate champions. We've got a long history of progressive leadership. Here, at a place known as The People's House, we've passed groundbreaking legislation on gay marriage, farm to plate, businesses for good, and universal health care. We've got a strong sense of community, a deeply egalitarian spirit, and a motto which says, "Freedom and Unity."

Unlike, say, New Hampshire, which has the motto, "Live Free or Die," we understand that our freedom comes directly from the strength of our communities. It comes from our ability to engage, with civility and respect, those with whom we disagree. Vermonters know how to listen. Vermonters know how to care. Vermonters know how to work hard. And Vermonters know how to lead.

Small though we are, we know that climate leadership is our task, our holy calling. We've been blessed with the great fortune to live in this beautiful, inspiring, utterly unique landscape. We understand on a deep level that we live hand in hand with each other, and hand in wing in paw in fin in claw with all the other creatures around us. We know how vast, interconnected, delicate, and alive our ecosystem is. And we know it's our responsibility, as smart, visionary, committed human creatures, to keep that ecosystem whole.

We also know it's not like this in the rest of the country. We know how divisive and broken many other places are. We know how much action is NOT being taken, we know how many lies are being spread.

We know that Vermonters are here to be a beacon of hope for the rest of the country and for the planet. We are here to make the impossible possible. We are here to do the hard, right, and righteous work. We are here to accept nothing less than wholeness, sustainability, resilience, and justice. We are here with fierce urgency. We are here to demand immediate action. We will accept nothing less than everything. We are here to ignite and inspire. We are here to mend the world.

Alternative Commencement Address
Worcester Polytechnic Institute
Written in response to a graduation speaker fracas at WPI and posted on YouTube - much to WPI students' delight.

My name is Kathryn Blume. I'm a writer, performer, and climate activist, and I wanted to express my solidarity with the students and faculty at Worcester Polytechnic Institute who are opposing Exxon/Mobil CEO Rex Tillerson as their graduation speaker.

While I realize the remarkable Richard Hineberg has offered himself as an alternative to Mr. Tillerson, I thought maybe Mr. Hineberg could use a little backup. And if you *are* all forced to listen to Mr. Tillerson, then perhaps having a number of alternative commencement addresses might, in the end, be a bit of a balm to the unanticipated controversy marking the end of your time at WPI.

First off, I want to say, keep up the good work! And don't be too troubled by what happens on graduation day.

If you care about the future of this planet, if you care about shining the light of truth into the dark caverns of denial and dishonesty, if you care about figuring out how humanity can possibly live in health and wholeness on this tiny blue dot in the infinite blackness of the universe, then this is only one in a long line of battles you're going to be fighting.

Regardless of what happens right now, no matter who'll be offering up their droplets of wisdom come commencement, you have already signed up to be holy warriors for the planet. You've already committed your passion and your spirit and your honor to tending the welfare of the world, to mending what's broken, and you'll be at it for the rest of your lives. So have patience, have perspective, and have vision.

Have a vision of who you want to be, what role you want to play in this great epic. Because it is a great epic. It's the most rugged, robust, high stakes story humanity has ever played out. And you, right now, in your struggle, are an integral part of the narrative. You're as mighty and archetypal a protagonist as Frodo Baggins or Harry Potter. And, much like them, you didn't ask to be born in this time of overwhelming planetary peril.

But born you were, and the voices of justice and responsibility singing carols in your soul demand that you step up, demand that you take a gigantic risk. They demand, without cease, that you act. They demand it - because it's the only right thing to do.

Now, as a theater artist, it's practically reflexive for me to fall into casting the heros and villains in a story. And it seems all to easy to identify who's who in this particular tale. Rex Tillerson is an easy choice for a malevolent, snake-snouted Voldemort. But I'd like to caution against vilifying Mr.

Tillerson or, for that matter, anyone in the WPI administration who may have invited or supported him.

We cannot fall into an us versus them mentality. The world is too small, the climate crisis too acute, and the time too short to get divisive and combative. For one, it takes energy away from our work of visioning and crafting the world we DO want to live in. But more importantly, it causes us to lose our compassion. Yes, Mr. Tillerson is the CEO of a company which has helped ravage the planet while raking in astronomical profits. Yes, he's funded over 39 climate change-denying organizations. Yes, he's a prominent member of an industry which has bought out the US Congress, and funded the slaughter of any useful climate legislation.

But really, like the oil he peddles, he is a creature of the Jurassic, mired in an old paradigm - one of infinite growth, endless consumption, and of sacrificing everything we hold dear on the altar of maximum profit. It's a paradigm which is being depleted as rapidly as this planet's reserves of fossil fuel. And powerful as they seem - both man and paradigm - neither of them will last. Nor will the oil for that matter. So we should not waste our energies on hate.

Not to mention the fact that, like it or not, we are all products of this paradigm. Those of us born and raised in the developed world have grown up in a culture and economy utterly permeated with and completely dependent upon a cheap, abundant supply of fossil fuel. None of our lives, as they are now, would have been possible without what Mr. Tillerson is selling.

And so, as hard as Mr. Tillerson is fighting to keep his wealth, power, and crumbling world view intact, we have to fight equally hard to extract ourselves from our fossil-fueled lives. We have to stare our economic systems, our expectations for our future - indeed our very manner of existing on this planet - in the face. We have to question everything. We have to reexamine what's necessary, what's preferable, and what's sustainable. And we have to make radical changes as fast as we possibly can.

Because humanity is facing a two-headed axe - a labrys, if you will - of climate change and peak oil. They're real, they're happening now, and there is no escaping the harsh, urgent truth that the planet's capacity to support us as we figure out what to do is rapidly unraveling.

We have very little time.

Not only that, but many modern thinkers will tell you that we, as a species, have lost any sense of future, that we have an expectation of landing, sooner or later, in some form of apocalyptic dystopia. And the way things are going, many people might say we'll be walking Cormac McCarthy's Road much, much sooner than any of us expected.

Well, that's one form the story can take. However, we also have something else. We have humanity's magnificent adaptability, ingenuity, and creativity. We have a great desire to survive, and thrive, and live beautiful, meaningful, purposeful lives. We have the quirky characteristic, as articulated by Jeff Bridges playing an alien in the movie "Starman," that we are at our best when things are at their worst.

We may have taken all that oil we found and totally messed up the planet, but we certainly didn't mean to! And think about what we managed to create! Airplanes and laptops and motorcycles and lycra and the Hubble telescope and contact lenses and CDs and superglue! It's been a great party!

Now we just have to take all our infinitely innovative capacities and harness them in service of a galactically massive, wildly challenging to imagine socio-economic-cultural-spiritual transformation. Sure, it's overwhelming. Seemingly impossible. But, as humans, doing the impossible seems to be our speciality.

Fast as the clock is ticking, we're not dead yet. This planet is still an exquisitely beautiful place. And it's the only one we've got. It is utterly worth fighting for. Our lives are worth fighting for. Our love for the world and our love for each other are worth fighting for.

So have more faith and courage and compassion than you can measure. Don't be daunted by the task at hand. Don't even wonder if it's possible. Just go forth and heal the world. Don't let anyone or anything stand in your way. Be the crazily creative love-warrior heros of the story. In fact, you already are. And it's a beautiful thing to see.

Dancing to the Beat of the Great Green Heart
Keynote address for the
Vermont Energy and Climate Action Network Annual Conference

You know, I often get brought in to do talks like this when presenters feel like they've got a pointed-yet-slightly-inchoate need for...*something*. Often they're not sure quite what. Not something informative, exactly. Or even something practically useful.

Which is good, because I'm more of an idea gal, and I have no idea how practically useful I could be to anybody.

I know I'm being brought in partly for the entertainment value, but I also know whatever speech I come up with needs to be more than *just* entertaining. It needs to be inspiring. It needs to have surprise. And substance. And sex appeal. I'm serious! I met a Danish woman once who said to me, "The problem with climate change and peak oil is that they are not funny and they are not sexy. You have GOT to make them funny and you have GOT to make them sexy!"

So, no pressure right?

One thing I do know is that a good keynote needs some visuals, and I've been wracking my brains for something that isn't Power Point because let's be honest here. Power Point? Bleh.

And then recently, I went to a concert given by some performers from remote, low-lying Pacific island nations which are being rapidly inundated by rising sea levels. So you know that was a heartwarming and hopeful evening.

One of the islands, Tuvalu, has been on my mind for years because I have this one-woman show I do called *The Boycott* about the First Lady of the US launching a sex strike to combat global warming, and one of the characters is a climate activist from Tuvalu.

Before this concert, the only time I'd ever met an Actual Tuvaluan was when I took my show to Copenhagen for those fateful UN climate talks. Tuvalu had its own info booth, and the minute I saw it, I went over to the guy behind the counter and said, "Hi! I am a big fan of your country!" and I handed him a postcard for my show, which was a picture of two polar bears humping on a tiny ice floe in the middle of the ocean with a caption reading, "No sex please, we're melting."

It turned out that Info Booth Guy was actually an official delegate who was there to check his email and who looked at me like I was a very small dog trying to vigorously mate with his leg.

Fortunately, the performing Tuvaluans liked me a better than Official Delegate Guy, and gave me this garland to prove it. So there. Visuals.

Tuvalu is less than a mile wide and its highest point is about 6′ above sea level, and climate change (or as a friend calls it, "this whole climate thingy") has already progressed so far that they're pretty much screwed. A little atoll where one guy's grandfather used to live is completely gone, and someday, in the not-too-distant future, there won't be a Tuvalu anymore. And they all know it.

The young man who gave me this garland said, "We are warriors. No matter how high the ocean gets, we will stay. We will die for our country."

I hugged him and made a big point of saying that I knew all about Tuvalu, and so did a lot of my friends, and we were thinking about them and doing our best to try and address this whole climate thingy... But he stopped me and said, "It's not just us. It's everybody."

Of course he was right. I was a little embarrassed. Because - despite being a die-hard climate activist and dedicating the bulk of my life to the cause, despite talking and thinking and writing and acting and organizing and blogging and facebooking and tweeting about this all the damn time, I somehow managed to forget, had the luxury of forgetting, just for a moment, that it's all of us.

It's everybody. You and me and everyone we know and everything we cherish. It's even everything we hate or which annoys or plagues us or gives us indigestion or night sweats.

It's everything. All our systems, assumptions, values. It's all our relationships, expectations, traditions. It's our sense of possibility. It's how we eat, work, travel, play, educate. It's what we learn, what we believe, what we dream of, what we choose to hold close, what we are forced to cast away. Even our hope. Everything is going to change. Everything is already changing. Certainly those of you from the more Irene-soaked portions of Vermont are pretty conscious of that.

* * *

Now, as you can see, I'm trying to be pointedly poetic here without getting into all the increasingly grim news from COP17 in Durban or citing freakout-worthy details from reports by the Intergovernmental Panel on Climate Change and the International Energy Agency. I mean I can. And if you don't behave yourselves, maybe I will.

But, you're a pretty savvy bunch, otherwise you wouldn't be sitting here. Many of you are underpaid and/or overworked professionals who deal with this stuff every day. Many of you are volunteers willing to give up your free time to sit around kitchen tables on cold February nights and figure out how to retrofit your town hall or get your neighbors to change their lightbulbs. And that is all, as our friend Jon Stewart would say, "Aweeesommme!"

But I want to reframe, or refocus, our attention. Because what we've got going on right now is a major confluence of challenges and opportunities. It's an unprecedented historic moment which Vermont (and by Vermont, I mean all of you) - which Vermont is uniquely suited to address. First, though, let's lay out the context:

Challenges. Well, there's the accelerating pace of climate change and our increasingly volatile and destructive weather systems; there's disrupted food production, infrastructure impact, millions of refugees, drought, ice melt, unraveling ecosystems, mass extinctions, the acidification of the rising ocean, etc, etc... In sum: real, urgent, scary, bad.

There's the destabilizing effect of peak oil and rampant, no holds barred, last ditch fossil fuel development with mountaintop removal and tar sands and fracking and deep ocean drilling and gigantic, untended spills. There's the political and economic power of the heavily subsidized and barely regulated fossil fuel industry, which is reaping more profits than any other industry in the history of money, and which pretty much has the US Congress in its back pocket.

Or, rather, I should say which has Congress in *his* back pocket, because the Supreme Court has told us corporations are people, free to inject as much money as they want into our democratic process. And they do. And it works.

There's our dominant economic model, based on principles of infinite growth, endless resource extraction, trashing of the commons, and operating on the assumption that we'll have cheap oil in perpetuity.

There's also the paradigm that maximizing economic growth is the most important thing our society can accomplish, and we pretty much have carte blanche to do whatever it takes to achieve it. Whenever growth comes into conflict with any other values we might hold, we tend to shrug our shoulders and say, "It's just business" or "It's for the economy."

There's oil itself, a totally miraculous substance that's been completely massaged into every aspect and system of our lives. And there's no 1:1 replacement available. No renewables can do an easy equivalent of what oil and other fossil fuels can do, which is why the changes we need to make are both so hard and so fundamentally difficult to even imagine.

Then there's the challenge of keeping hold of the narrative and movement momentum in the face of the deniers, the doubters, the apathetics, the corporate-owned media, and the myth of technological salvation.

However...we are Vermont. We're practically the Shire. And we are a powerful force for good in the world. We're more than that. We're an inspirational model. We know, in many ways, how to Get Stuff Done.

So, if ever there was a critical moment in the history of humanity to step it up and change the Business As Usual model, now would be the time, and Vermont would be the place. Because the world can't do it without the United States, and someone has got to show the rest of the country what's possible.

* * *

The thing is, though, we have to step it up, too. We have to take a look at what our Business As Usual assumptions are, and upend them completely.

And what might some of those be?

Well, a lot of you are town energy committee people. And that often involves working with your selectboards on nuts-and-bolts projects to implement incremental change. You host retrofitting workshops, and get solar on your schools, and promote alternative transportation solutions.

And that's all valuable, important, necessary work. The problem is that it's tiny, little, step-by-step change. It's not even close to enough. Which means if you've been feeling like slow progressive improvements aren't working, you're right! If you feel like you don't have enough people working with you, you're right. If you even think there aren't enough people here today, you're right. We should be in the thousands. We should be legion.

Plus, the current model you're working in isolates energy from every other aspect of how our communities function. So those of you on your town energy committee, you're stuck with the wrong name. You're not actually on your town's energy committee. You're on your town's LIFE committee. You're on the committee which can help shape every aspect of your community's future, and which needs to do it holistically, boldly, and with a wide open eye towards the common good.

More Business As Usual Assumptions can be found in some of the public response to the state energy plan. The Associated Industries of Vermont, the Vermont Energy Partnership, and other organizations recently held a press conference complaining that the energy plan focuses on climate change, renewable energy, and efficiency to such an extent that they have become goals in and of themselves (to which I say, "Ummm...*yeah!*").

The Associated Industries of Vermont said, "Our concern is with any framework for legislation or rules that will complicate things for the economy, that will make energy more expensive, less reliable or otherwise raise obstacles to commerce."

I'm not vilifying the AIV here. I'm really not. I get that they're concerned about a healthy economic environment. We all are. The problem is that they're mired in a false paradigm -

the absurd idea that environmental health and economic growth are at odds with each other. They're mired in the ridiculous idea that true economic health can be achieved without environmental health. And even more than that, they're mired in the old - nay, jurassic - paradigm that endless growth is not only good and desirable, but *possible*. Because it's not. At least not if you want a nice, healthy planet to live on.

Another Business As Usual Assumption can be found in the energy plan itself, with its interim reliance on natural gas, and long term reliance on forest biomass - burning lots and lots and lots of trees - as acceptable sources of electricity. To which I say, "Frack that!"

I submit to you that we need to draw a line in the sand and say we will not derive our energy from anything which adversely impacts the human or natural communities from which it's extracted, and which releases particulates, greenhouse gasses, and other toxins into our environment. As both of those energy sources do.

I challenge us to say no - even if it threatens a short term gap. In fact *precisely* if it threatens a short term gap. Because that gap can serve as a potent motivator for finding truly green, truly sustainable solutions. That gap can be a creative gap, a highly pressurized crucible for innovation. That gap is part of our moral obligation to - for once - champion the health of the planet over our own sense of entitled need.

Basically, It's time to move from incremental, predictable change to fundamental, breathtaking change, and you, each and every one of you are fundamental change agents. Each and every one of you have the power to make an enormous impact on the long term well being of the places and the people you care about.

* * *

And that's really what this is about. I titled this talk Dancing to the Beat of the Great Green Heart, and I meant it. We do this work, in spite of all the odds and worrisome statistics and grim predictions and cold February kitchen tables because of our deep, shining emerald love for the world and for the people in it.

We are the children of an utterly miraculous planet, a tiny aquamarine jewel floating in a sea of black velvet infinity. We are her warriors and her guardians and we do this work because our hearts demand it. And we look at all those odds and statistics and predictions and we say, much like Gimli in Lord of the Rings, "Small chance of success. Certainty of death. What are we waiting for?"

Really, there is no more waiting. This is the moment, a time when, all over the world, folks just like us are reinventing the democratic process. They're building community and fostering widespread participation. They believe that true power comes from the will of the people, and their job is to bring enough people to the table to have an impact.

They're teaching us about determination and commitment, and they're proving the truth of Paul Hawken's statement that, "If you look at the science about what is happening on earth and aren't pessimistic, you don't understand the data. But if you meet the people who are working to restore this earth and the lives of the poor, and you aren't optimistic, you haven't got a pulse."

* * *

So, back to Vermont. We've got this great Governor, one of the few in the country who will not only speak the words "climate change" but shout it from the rooftops. We've got a Congressional delegation that's the envy of all non-crazy people everywhere. We've got brilliant, committed officials like Liz Miller and Deb Markowitz - whom I love because she's even shorter than I am - and all the dedicated folks who serve under them and who've been waiting for *years* for the green light to really DO something positive and far-reaching for the state.

We've got hard working groups like VNRC and VPIRG and VEIC and 350VT and all the Transition Towns. We've got organic farmers and permaculture innovators and slow money proponents and sustainability educators and green transportation advocates and socially responsible business

leaders and all the colleges and universities with
environmental studies programs, and lots of really great,
locally made cheese! I could go on forever about everything
we've got in our tool belt, but I'll just add one more to the list.
We've got this energy plan.

It's an exhaustively researched, ambitious, well considered,
deeply inclusive document. And, by its very nature, by the
historical context in which it exists, it doesn't go nearly far
enough. It can't. Because what we really need is stop
emitting greenhouse gasses. Completely. Right now. Today.
Which means stop using fossil fuels. Completely. Right now.
Today. We need to move people around, we need to feed,
house, clothe, educate, employ, heal, entertain, and sustain
everyone we know AND increase our communities' resilience
to all manner of environmental, economic, political, and social
disruptions without burning another drop of oil or whiff of
gas or scrap of coal. Ever.

And we all know that's impossible.

But I will go out on a limb here and say that it's still got to be
our North Star, our guiding principle, our Green Golden Rule.
It's got to be the rigorously, impossibly high goal towards
which we strive because anything short of that will get us
nowhere.

And this is where all of you come back into the story. Because
as remarkable as this administration is, as fortunate as we are

to have all these amazing leaders, and as important as the work you do is, Vermont exists in the real world - a world with powerful forces which operate in direct opposition to what we're trying to accomplish, and which work vigorously to undermine our campaign for wholeness, for survival.

Which means your job is to say to your leaders, "We've got your back. We'll hold strong and help you push forward." But you also have to say to your leaders, "We've got your feet - and we've got 'em in the fire. We're going to remind you - and keep reminding you - of the urgency of these times, the intensity of our aspirations and the uncompromising rigor of our goals. We're going to hold you to your highest ideals because nothing less will do."

Of course we also have to say that to each other, with great love and unswerving compassion. It's so easy to slip, to falter, to slack, to forget, to despair, and to tire. It's easy to burn out and get overwhelmed by the might and money of the opposition and the momentum of The Way Things Are. It's easy to get cowed by those times when you start telling the hard truth about climate change and peak oil and why our current models of everything cannot continue, and have people get kind of wiggy on you - even if they're fundamentally on your side.

It's like a conversation we had in Charlotte recently about getting solar trackers for the town, and you'd hear some people say, "Well, of course I support solar power. I just don't want to have to look at those hideous things." Or when I gave a talk about climate and peak oil to the Women Business Owner's Network, and one gal said, very honestly, "I don't want to hear about this. It's too scary."

Of course it's scary. It scares the crap out of me. I heard McKibben say once that the first time he cried about climate change was in Copenhagen during COP15, and I thought he was either nuts or lying because I cry about it all the time.

But we simply have to, as my southern friend Hayley says, pull on our big girl panties and deal. And part of how we deal, part of how we get brave and bold and audacious and feisty and draw those hard lines in the sand is by turning to each other.

We need each other the way good neighbors need each other, the way family needs each other. We need to be people who can borrow stuff from each other, stuff like ideas and strength and creativity and determination and emotional resilience. I have a borrowing relationship like that with my friend Barbarina.

Barbarina is a remarkable climate activist who has the preternatural ability to read all the scary books and articles and watch all the scary documentaries, absorb and remember all that information, and then get up and say, "Ok. What's next?" I can't do that. So Barbarina screens a lot of information for me, gives me the salient details, and then I write funny, pithy, pointed remarks about it all, give them back to her, and she uses that language when she goes to lobby Congress. We call it the Symbiosis of the Petite World-Saving Amazons.

* * *

So, to wrap things up, I want to leave you with a few sprinkles of borrowable ideas and a few bits of green-hearted encouragement:

Talk to your elected officials - at all levels of government - and talk to them repeatedly. I know there can be reticence to get involved in electoral politics, but A) this is no time to be dainty, B) Vermont is one of those few places where we have top-to-bottom access and C) we can make a difference just by showing up. Show up more than once and you can make a BIG difference. A few calls or a couple of meetings can change a vote, or radically alter a piece of legislation.

And given the Energy Plan, there's going to be significant legislation coming along which will need all the attention and bolstering it can get. There will probably be legislative feet needing to be held to the fire. If you need help or more information, Joey Miller at VNRC is your point gal. She'll let you know what's going on and she'll show you the ropes for how to get involved.

Collaborate with your Town's Transition initiative if you've got one, or read up on the Transition model and methodology if you don't. Take a weekend Training for Transition workshop. The Transition model is all about building partnerships, strengthening relationships, and harnessing the inherent wisdom, skills, and creativity of your community as we move into a post-carbon world.

If you're feeling super climate-feisty, Vermont now has the country's first state-level 350 organization, and they're going to be putting a lot of time and attention into the Energy Plan. A major lynchpin of their approach is making sure that the solutions we come up with - clean energy and transportation, energy efficient buildings, green jobs, healthy forests, abundant local food - are solutions for *all* Vermonters. So if you're concerned about the social justice component of this work, they're a great group to talk to.

Have fun. Sing. Dance. Play. Tell fabulously visionary stories about our remarkable, positive future. Like I said, we're talking major gigantic colossal unbelievably huge whole systems transformation here, and that takes innovation, joy, hope, celebration, moxie and a whole heap of derring-do. It takes holding each other when times get hard and celebrating all the little victories which come your way.

Live and work from your great green heart. Focus on the things you care most deeply about. After all, anger, fear, and frustration are like lust. They're great short term fuels for getting you into a relationship or a cause or a movement. But it's love and devotion which keep you there.

Over the years I've asked a lot of people who are deep sustainability practitioners how we do this. How do we keep looking into the void, how do we keep fighting the fight, how do we keep from getting apocalyptic in our thinking? And the two answers which keep coming up are build your social networks (and they mean real world friends, not Facebook and Twitter) and plant a garden. I love those answers. I love that I keep hearing them. Recently, I found them reflected in a beautiful poem by Gary Snyder. And it's what I'll leave you with:

For the Children

The rising hills, the slopes,
of statistics
lie before us.
the steep climb
of everything, going up,
up, as we all
go down.

In the next century
or the one beyond that,
they say,
are valleys, pastures,
we can meet there in peace

if we make it.

To climb these coming crests
one word to you, to
you and your children:

stay together
learn the flowers
go light

www.ingramcontent.com/pod-product-compliance
Lightning Source LLC
Chambersburg PA
CBHW061121110426
R18123600001B/R181236PG42736CBX00001B/1